Switzerland
Unwrapped

SWITZERLAND UNWRAPPED

Exposing the Myths

Mitya New

I.B. Tauris Publishers
LONDON · NEW YORK

Published in 1997 by I.B.Tauris & Co Ltd,
Victoria House, Bloomsbury Square, London WC1B 4DZ

In the United States and Canada distributed by
St Martin's Press, 175 Fifth Avenue, New York NY 10010

A full CIP record for this book is available from the British
Library

A full CIP record for this book is available from the Library of
Congress

Set in Monotype Sabon and Univers by Ewan Smith, London
Printed and bound in Great Britain by WBC Ltd, Bridgend,
Mid Glamorgan

ISBN 1 86064 300 0

CONTENTS

ACKNOWLEDGEMENTS

I would like to thank the interviewees for making this book possible. Without them and the time they sacrificed to talk to me, as well as the encouragement and suggestions some of them gave, the book would not have been possible.

At Reuters I am indebted to Graham Williams for his support, David Christian-Edwards for his encouragement and for pointing out errors in the manuscript and to Albert Schmieder for helpful suggestions and stimulating ideas during the early stages of the project.

Michael Ferster took the time to read a draft version of the manuscript and made important suggestions for improvements. Peter Studer at DRS Swiss television gave valuable comments and ideas which set me on the right track from the very beginning. Colleagues of his in the '10 vor 10' news programme kindly searched through archives and provided a video recording and text transcript of an important interview.

Kostya provided an invaluable suggestion that bridged a difficult obstacle, Nikolai always showed a useful interest in the project, Christa and Christopher never failed in their support, encouragement and important criticism. Gisela and Martin gave kind support.

Lastly, and most importantly, Martina suggested the idea and believed in me.

NOTE

The opinions expressed in this book are solely those of the author and do not in any way represent opinions of Reuters news agency.

INTRODUCTION

'You want to understand Switzerland? Go to a *Schwingfest*; that's where you'll see the real Switzerland,' the man had said. And so I did. The distant but gradually growing roar of the crowd, as I strode up the road through the forest with a stream of people, heightened the expectation. The sunbeams shone through the leafy cover, and all around me children were dressed in the folk costumes that their parents were also wearing – tight, black or red waistcoats with silver buttons and fine, colourful embroidery, the women in long, dark, ceremonial dresses, some with wings and ornate head-dresses. The forest thinned and at the entrance to the clearing – a grassy glade surrounded by hills and trees on all sides – tickets were being sold, in this age of plastic and prefabrication, from small wooden huts the size of public telephone boxes.

On the left, on the way to the arena, a group of men and women in traditional dress yodelled from a makeshift stage. The audience, lying on the grass, sitting on half-buried boulders or standing, listened appreciatively, ignoring the crescendos from the ring. Nearby, an old man with a bushy, white beard bent gingerly from the waist to pick up the end of his long alpenhorn. He put his lips to the mouthpiece, puffed his cheeks, which turned a bright red, and a soft, deep, sonorous tone filled the air.

At the top rim of the arena, a natural gladiator's pit enclosed on two sides by the steep rise of the hill, the crowd stood shoulder to shoulder. Below people sat on long planks, fastened to short legs embedded in the sloping ground. The colours in the arena immediately overwhelmed the eye. Five rings of light yellow, almost white sawdust were spread out on the green grass. At each ring two judges sat at a simple wooden table, marking the points the wrestlers scored. One of them manually rotated a wooden scoreboard fixed

on a long pole and showing the participant numbers of the competitors in the ring. The wrestlers, writhing in the sawdust, were
either dressed all in white or in dark, chequered shirts and dark
trousers. All of them wore light-brown shorts, made of sacking
and fastened with a leather belt, over their trousers.

The spectators, mainly men, were focusing on one fight in a ring
in the far corner. Two wrestlers, crouching shoulder to shoulder,
with sweat streaming down their faces, and sand-caked hands and
burly forearms gripping the opponent's sacking shorts, struggled to
gain an advantage. Suddenly, with surprising speed, one of the
heavily-built fighters stood upright, lifting the other off the ground
and then, swinging and falling to one side in a single movement,
thudded down on top of him, pinning his shoulders to the ground.
Thousands of voices shouted their approval and then gradually,
after several minutes, the clamour subsided to an excited murmur.

This form of wrestling is as Swiss as sumo is Japanese. It is
something the Swiss take pride in – a sport that is exclusively
theirs, that only they understand. But is it any more or less the
real Switzerland than the *Kaesemeister* (cheese master) who, at his
dairy in the Emmental Valley, remembers how his family has long
been involved in dairy farming and cheesemaking? Then, as now,
the dairy farmers of the surrounding countryside would deliver
the fresh, unpasteurised milk to the dairy before dawn to be made
into cheese and butter. Then, as now, the cheese master knew each
of the farmers supplying the milk personally. This is the heart of
Switzerland's dairy country, where old women armed with pitch-
forks and dressed completely in black still work the land.

What about the local government official in charge of the
nuclear fall-out shelters in Zurich, the country's largest city? Proud-
ly he heaves open the massive, one-foot-thick concrete door of one
of the city's 70 public bunkers and then leads the way through an
ante-chamber where, he explains, the contaminated would be able
to scrub off radioactive material before entering the complex. He
describes how Switzerland began building the bunkers in the early
1960s at the height of the Cold War and still requires all new
residential buildings to have shelters in the cellars, equipped with
air filters. The last three pages of Swiss telephone directories advise
citizens that bunkers must be ready for occupation at a moment's
notice because of the danger of unexpected attack and tell them
to take non-perishable provisions along. 'To be quite honest, we

would only operate on people here if there was a 90 per cent chance of survival,' he says, in a show of worldly cold-heartedness, as he gestures towards the surgical facilities. 'We couldn't waste time on marginal cases.'

Switzerland is a country of four languages and many more dialects; three cultures that at times seem to tie the people more to neighbouring countries than to bind them together; 26 cantons which often command fierce loyalties and trigger bitter political conflicts which, however, are restrained by a commitment to consensus; extraordinary economic wealth that has replaced miserable poverty which was widespread barely a century ago; and only seven million people. It is also a country that, perhaps more than any other, is tightly wrapped in clichés – clichés about neutrality, banks and gnomes, mountains, chocolate and cuckoo clocks.

Certainly some of the clichés appear to have foundation. Lingering, dormant suspicions, that Swiss banks have been holding money deposited by Jews who subsequently died in the Nazi Holocaust, burst into life in 1995 following the release of British and US archive records and claims by the World Jewish Congress that Swiss banks were still hoarding billions of dollars in unclaimed assets of Holocaust victims. A 1996 British Foreign Office memorandum,[1] suggesting that Swiss banks had purchased gold plundered by Nazi Germany during the Second World War but returned only a fraction after 1945, fanned the flames of international outrage and revived the image of the duplicitous and amoral Swiss banker.

But unwrap the clichés and often a reality is revealed that is as surprising to outsiders as it is disturbing to the Swiss. Much has been made in Switzerland during the first half of the 1990s of the crisis of national identity – a collective soul-searching for Switzerland's roots, the core national values that hold the country together. The discussion came, not coincidentally, at a time when the country was riven by the question of whether to abandon its isolation and move closer to the rest of Europe.

In the spring of 1992 the government had deposited an application in Brussels for membership of the European Community (EC) and, with the benefit of hindsight, it is clear this step provoked a popular backlash against the government. Neutrality was under threat. The government was going against the very maxim that all Swiss children have drummed into them in school – Switzerland's interests have always been best preserved by avoiding foreign alliances. The issue came to a head with a referendum on – what many saw as the first step on the slippery slope leading to the EC – the government's decision to join the European Economic Area (EEA), a free trade area linking the EC and the European Free Trade Association (EFTA). After an unprecedentedly bitter campaign, in which both opponents and proponents accused each other of high treason, Swiss voters rejected membership of the EEA in December 1992.

The outcome of this referendum is still reverberating through Switzerland. It has heightened and revived a long-standing historical animosity between the German-speaking majority in the east of the country and the Francophone west. It has also left a gulf between the political and economic establishment which remains determined to join Europe and much of the electorate which is equally determined not to.

But the questions over national identity go deeper and have existed longer than the vote over Europe. They touch on the institution of the army, the banks, the treatment of gypsies and, even further back in history, Switzerland's policies towards the Jews during the Second World War. Perhaps the clearest sign of the national self-questioning is the revival in the 1990s of an old debate over the origins of the Swiss confederation. Most historians accept that the Swiss folk hero William Tell was a mythical figure who was never forced to shoot an apple off his son's head with a crossbow as cruel punishment for failing to salute a hat perched on a pole by the local Austrian Habsburg ruler. But there is considerably more debate over subsequent developments.

Although Tell himself did not exist, a revolt against the Habsburgs, that Tell is supposed to have provoked, is believed by some historians to be fact. A revisionist school, however, disagrees, saying that there is no evidence, neither historical nor archaeological, of any such rebellion against the Habsburgs, who then controlled the Swiss territories. An alliance signed on 1 August 1291 between Uri, Schwyz and Nidwalden – the three core cantons of Switzerland – was not the basis for the revolt, as the traditional interpretation claims, but a search for mutual security following the death of the Habsburg ruler, King Rudolf. And any number of other alliances between different towns and regions, both before and after 1291, were no less important. Furthermore, the revisionists argue, the traditional interpretation is particularly nefarious because it has laid the basis for a myth that the Swiss fought for and defended their independence and liberty. This myth lies at the heart of the Swiss view of their neutrality, the neutrality that so many of them saw threatened in 1992 by closer ties with Europe and that lies so deeply embedded in the culture of the country.[2]

But regardless of the questions of what Switzerland is, whether it should change and if so in which direction, the *Schwingers* will continue to heave in the sawdust, the *Kaesemeisters* to guide the wheels of cheese through the fermentation process and the fall-out shelter warden to check the bunkers are adequately provisioned. This book presents Switzerland through the eyes of these people – the people living and working in the country, experiencing difficulties and successes, disappointments and joys. Each of their accounts represents a part of the mosaic of the country. Perhaps it will help to dispel some clichés; equally, perhaps, it will confirm others.

Notes

1. The British Foreign Office announced on 10 September 1996 that Switzerland had returned only a tenth of some $500 million worth of German gold (worth some $6.5 billion at today's prices) to Allied powers at the end of the Second World War (Reuters news service, 10 September 1996).

2. An original parchment with the text of the pact of 1291 is preserved as a kind of federal charter in an archive in the canton of Schwyz. Switzerland is officially said to date from 1291 and 1 August is a national holiday. The Ruetli meadow, where the signing is supposed to have taken place, is an area of tremendous national reverence.

Chapter 1

SWITZERLAND AND THE JEWS

Das Boot ist voll. The boat is full. No phrase more clearly expresses the official Swiss attitude towards Jews fleeing Nazi persecution to Switzerland during the late 1930s and the Second World War.[1]

Switzerland, neutral, home to the International Red Cross and proud of its role as a haven for refugees – from the Huguenots in the seventeenth century to pacifists in the twentieth century – gave Jews fleeing Nazi persecution a far from welcoming reception. Borders were closed and Jews turned back. Refugees were only accepted once Jewish organisations had guaranteed they would foot the bill for their stay. And, in a measure that showed bureaucratic efficiency had won over moral imperatives, Berne secretly and successfully pressed the Nazi government to mark German Jewish passports with a distinguishing stamp so that Swiss border officials could more easily pick out Jews at the frontier.

However, as Paul Grueninger's story shows (although one of the most prominent sympathisers with the refugees' situation, he was far from alone) some Swiss were prepared to ignore Berne's directives and help Jewish refugees, who they knew from newspapers or from hearsay were fleeing in genuine fear of their lives.

It is easy to claim Swiss policy was evidence of latent Swiss anti-Semitism and, to a degree, this is true. Since the Middle Ages the Jewish Diaspora had suffered no less anti-Semitic prejudice in the confederation than elsewhere in Europe. And shortly before the Second World War the chief of the Swiss federal police could say to the German ambassador in Berne that Switzerland must guard against a flood of Jews 'whom Switzerland has as little use for as Germany'.[2] But this explanation is incomplete. Swiss authorities genuinely feared the country would be overwhelmed by an uncontrollable flood of Jewish refugees if they did not close the borders. The Depression of the early 1930s was still a vivid memory, and large numbers of immigrants would bring unemployment and social tensions. And since few countries were willing to accept German Jews who had escaped to Switzerland, the government feared becoming Europe's repository for Jewish refugees.

Ultimately Switzerland's policy towards the Jews was dictated by the precariousness of Swiss neutrality. The Swiss could not afford to provoke the ire of the increasingly powerful Nazi military regime. Shortly before and during the Second World War Swiss diplomats walked a tightrope between the Allied and Axis camps, seeking to offend neither but, equally, taking desperate care not to be seen to favour either. The policy made a mockery of Switzerland's traditional foreign policy of armed neutrality and led, inevitably, to compromises. The Swiss government's policy towards the Jews was one of these.

In this chapter Ruth Rhoduner, daughter of Paul Grueninger (the local police chief in the north-eastern canton of St Gallen) and now 72 years old, remembers how her father was punished for ignoring government policy and falsifying official records to save hundreds – possibly thousands – of Jews.

Jacques Picard, a revisionist Swiss historian who has researched Switzerland's policies towards the Jews and Germany before and during the Second World War, provides the historical background to the case of Paul Grueninger. Picard has sharply criticised Swiss foreign policy during this period as neither impartial nor neutral. He is also the author of an unpublished investigation into the fate of funds deposited in Switzerland by the racially, religiously and politically persecuted before and during the Second World War.

Notes

1. *Das Boot ist voll* is the title of a book by Swiss historian Alfred Haesler, analysing the roots of anti-Semitism in Switzerland and criticising Swiss government policy towards the Jews before and during the Second World War. Haesler, who was one of the first Swiss historians to write about this aspect of Switzerland's past, took his title from a speech by Swiss justice minister Eduard von Steiger, made in 1942, in which he warned that the Swiss 'lifeboat' was full and could not take any more refugees (Alfred Haesler, 1992, p. 122).

2. Chief of the police department in the Federal Justice Ministry, Dr Heinrich Rothmund (*Grueningers Fall*, Stefan Keller, 1993, p. 46).

PAUL GRUENINGER

Ruth Rhoduner

'I am not ashamed of my sentence. On the contrary I am proud of having saved hundreds of people in a difficult situation. My support for the Jews came from my Christian world view. If I was ever in a particularly difficult situation there was always a way out. I was graced with God's help in abundance.' (From address, written by Paul Grueninger for his own funeral.)

Ruth Rhoduner is 72 years old. Her husband died recently and she lives alone, apart from her small dog, in a top-floor flat in a small village close to the Austrian border and very near where her father spent most of his life following his dismissal. She speaks animatedly from a couch, her dog on her lap. Later she gets up to find documents and photographs of her father, which she spreads over the table in front of her. 'I don't have many documents or pictures left of my father. I gave most of them to the journalists who came to write stories about my father and they never returned them. I suppose I should have been more careful.' She is philosophical rather than bitter and is grateful that an interest is being shown in her father but feels it has come far too late.

Most of the Jewish refugees came over at a place called Diepold-sau, just a few kilometres from here. It was an ideal place for illegal crossings because of the re-routeing of the Rhine river, which runs along part of the border between Austria and Switzerland. A bend in the river was removed at the beginning of the twentieth century because it had caused a lot of flooding in the area. After the redirection a swampy area was left between the old river's course, where the Austrian border remained, and the new straightened

Rhine. It was swampland, with some bush and shrubs, and people who knew where to tread came across or were led across.

There were people helping them on the other side, including the Swiss Consul at Bregrenz who drove a few over in his car but was caught trying to lead a man across the border at night. We did not know at the time, but apparently word had got around among the refugees that this was the best escape route from Vorarlberg and it was one of the main escape routes from Austria. Some of the border guards were in on it as well and would know that at certain times of the day or night they should allow a particular group of people through without checking their papers.

This was in 1938 when Austria had became part of the German Reich following the Anschluss and when the Nazis were passing anti-Semitic laws in Austria. The people fleeing were predominantly Jewish, many of whom had earlier fled from Germany to Austria. They were coming over the border at Basle and other places in Switzerland as well, but thousands came over at Diepoldsau. Also this was a traditionally Jewish area. For years Jews had lived in this area on the Austrian side of the border; in fact, just across the border in Hohenems in Austria there is a Jewish cemetery.

They came over and then pretty quickly they were picked up by police officers and border patrols who should have sent them back. But many couldn't bring themselves to do that because they had heard enough of the situation in Germany and Austria to know they would be sending the Jews back to certain death in the concentration camps. Instead they would send them to police head-quarters at St Gallen or to the *Israelitische Fluechtlingshilfe* (Israeli Refugee Assistance), which was working together with the police. It kept records of all new arrivals.

My father was police chief for the canton of St Gallen and so he and his boss, Regierungsrat (government councillor) Valentin Keel, had to decide what to do with the refugees. Keel was the councillor responsible for the police department in the St Gallen *Regierungsrat* (government council). So several times a week my father and Keel, who had his office directly opposite my father's office on the same corridor, would see the Jews waiting anxiously on chairs in the corridor before being interviewed by my father. Sometimes the refugees went to the local office of the *Israelitische Fluechtlingshilfe* which would then call up the police in St Gallen asking what should be done with them. My father simply could not bring himself to send the people back because he knew, as many people in Switzerland had begun to realise by then, that they would probably be immediately carted off to concentration camps and almost certain death. I remember my father saying that he had often asked Keel: 'What shall we do with these people?' And Keel had replied: 'Well we can't just send them back, we'll have to see what we can do.' Later, however, Keel did not stand up for what he had said and done. He was the one who abandoned and betrayed my father and who claimed he hadn't known so many people were involved even though they had often been waiting outside the door of his office to see my father.

My family is not Jewish and has no Jewish roots. My father was brought up as a Protestant, although his father was a Catholic. His parents ran a cigar shop in St Gallen. There were Jews in St Gallen, with Jewish shops and Jewish children in the schools. But one could hardly tell them apart from non-Jews, unless perhaps by their names. There were Jewish children in my school and some from extremely orthodox families did not come to school on Saturdays because they were not allowed to travel, in observance of the Sabbath. But the Jews were not treated any differently from Catholics and Protestants; they were certainly not maltreated, disadvantaged or persecuted. Probably one would have helped people of other religions if they had been fleeing, but it happened to be the Jews – and we had heard and read in newspapers what was happening to them in Germany under Hitler.

There were three categories of Jewish refugees: first, those who already had money in Switzerland and who came here and lived on that money. Second, those who travelled on to other countries such as America, and who only stayed in Switzerland temporarily while in transit. The third category was those who arrived penniless and had nothing and nowhere to go. These Jews, however, were not a burden for the Swiss because the Jewish organisations in Switzerland paid for places for them to live and for their food and so on. Jewish groups organised a camp for them to stay in Diepoldsau or arranged hotel rooms for them. The camp in Diepoldsau was an old embroidery factory and there the refugees were given a bed to sleep on and something to eat. In Diepoldsau itself there were a few families who took some of the refugees into their homes or gave them jobs on the land to allow them to earn a few centimes. Some of them were able to work in restaurants. We did not have any Jews staying with us at home in St Gallen, but my mother gave some of the children, of which there were quite a few, little playthings and also gave a few clothes to some of the women.

Later during the War the Swiss government started interning Jews in government camps and made them work for their living. After the War most of the Jewish refugees left Switzerland, some to return to Austria or even Germany, but most emigrated to the new state of Israel. So there were few former Jewish refugees, who perhaps had been saved by my father, still left in Switzerland after the War. If more had stayed, perhaps they would have been able to speak up in my father's favour and help him after the War when things were going so badly for him.

There was no support or assistance from Jewish groups for my father during the War, but obviously the Jews had their own worries at that time. Everyone had a very hard time during the War. Very many Jews at this time left St Gallen and moved to western Switzerland, just to get away from the Austrian border where some people feared an attack from Germany would come. In 1940 we all feared a Nazi invasion.

The problems came for my father after the 18 August regulations from Berne which were very strict and said that all Jewish refugees coming into Switzerland without a visa must be sent back. There had been a number of divided refugee families where part of the family had managed to escape to Switzerland before the eighteenth, while the rest crossed over after that date. Once the new regulations had been introduced the head of the *Israelitische Fluechtlingshilfe* came to my father in desperation and said: 'What can we do? We can't send the mother back and keep the father and son here.'

So my father suggested that in cases of divided families the *Israelitische Fluechtlingshilfe* should falsify the arrival date of those who came after 18 August and bring it forward to before the eighteenth. It was this suggestion, this advice he gave to the *Israelitische Fluechtlingshilfe* that led to his dismissal and trial. I don't know why, perhaps they became scared, but the *Israelitische Fluechtlingshilfe* did little to help my father. They abandoned him and told the authorities they had falsified the records on my father's instructions.

The dismissal was very sudden at the beginning of 1939. My father left home one morning to walk to his office as he did every day. We lived in a service apartment in St Gallen, not far from the police headquarters. We were in the upper flat and another police-man lived in the lower apartment. My father had to walk through an old part of St Gallen, the only old part of the town that has been preserved, and through the gate to Klosterplatz where the government offices and police headquarters are. So my father arrived at police headquarters after his morning walk and wanted to go to work as normal. But he was stopped at the main entrance. There were two policemen at the door who said they couldn't let him enter because he had been suspended. He was never allowed into his office again, not even to pick up his personal belongings. These were brought to him at home not long after he was sus-pended. A couple of weeks later he was dismissed and a policeman came to our home and demanded my father's uniform and took it away. My mother was at home at the time and she always said afterwards that the loss of the uniform hurt her and my father the most.

Friends and relations said at the time: 'Surely they will reinstate you, they can't just throw you out like that!' The trial was post-poned and it took quite a long time to come to court. The verdict was sent by post and arrived one morning. It simply said that my father was guilty of ignoring federal regulations and of falsifying records. The sentence was really his dismissal, which was confirmed. There was also a 300-franc fine plus court costs. That meant that of all the money he had contributed to his pension scheme from his monthly salary very little was left when it was returned to him after the verdict. The whole business left him and his family penni-less, of course, for he had had no salary from the day he was dismissed and now there was also no pension. He did not appeal; he could not see the point. He felt that what he had done was right and that there was nothing more to be said or done.

The dismissal was in 1939 and my father was born in 1891, so he was 48 then, and by the time the verdict came he was 50 and in a very difficult situation financially. He looked desperately for work and found various odd jobs. But after his dismissal he never really ever found anything with which he could earn enough to look after his family adequately. Partly this was because times were difficult, of course, but partly it was also because everyone at that time feared an invasion by Hitler and nobody wanted to be associated with a saviour of the Jews should the Nazis occupy Switzerland.

The whole thing was also very difficult for my mother. I also have a sister who is 12 years younger than me and if it had not been for her I think my mother and father might have despaired. With her they had a task in life. Financially it was difficult, sometimes we did not know how we would get through the next day. My mother had a bit of money from her parents and my father also earned money now and then.

If my parents had had more money saved they could perhaps have gone into business, bought a stake in a small firm. My grandparents helped a little financially. I was at this time in Lausanne at a school of commerce and it was decided my grandmother would pay the fees for me to finish that year, but not the whole course. And then I came back and looked for a job in St Gallen; I could not find anything. Partly I faced the same difficulty as my father – I was tainted as a Jew-helper. I came back with a colleague from Lausanne and we both went to look for a job at the school of commerce in St Gallen where we had studied together before. We were interviewed by the school director and the next day she was offered a job and I was not. I am sure the director knew that giving me the job would have helped my parents' financial situation and that it was therefore much more important for me to get a job than it was for her.

Finally, my father asked a Jewish family, who had originally come to him when he was police chief begging for his assistance in the Jewish refugee problem, whether they could give me work. They gave me a job in their textile company. I earned a monthly wage of 120 francs, most of which went on the rent of our flat. My parents had already had to move out of their police service apartment while I was in Lausanne and had found another small flat in the town which cost 100 francs a month.

At first, before the verdict came, my father had hoped and believed he would be reinstated in the police force. Our friends and relatives thought so as well: 'They can't fire you for something like that.' Later he stopped hoping. He had originally been trained as a teacher, but following his dismissal and the trial he was also forbidden to work as a teacher. Only much, much later when he was 60 did he find a school which was prepared to employ him and by then the authorities were willing to give their approval.

Later my parents moved here to Au and lived in my grandmother's house. She was quite old and unable to live alone, and had a large house, which she could not look after on her own. So it made sense for all concerned. My mother looked after the house and my parents didn't have to pay any rent. This was where my father found a job as a teacher again. A friend of my grandmother's worked at a home for boys with education difficulties and he discovered my father was a fully-trained teacher. There was a severe shortage of school teachers after the War and the school asked him if he wanted to teach in the school, and the education authority, which had to approve the appointments of teachers, gave their permission. However, though the job didn't last long, from this time on he always managed to find work as a fill-in teacher in a number of different schools. The financial situation improved a little and he felt more fulfilled and satisfied with his life because he enjoyed working at his original career again and because he enjoyed being with children. He taught until he was about 70.

In 1968 I was working as a temporary assistant – a couple of hours a week on correspondence and other such things – for Staenderat (a member of the upper house of parliament) Dr Willi Rohner in Altstetten, who previously had been editor at the local newspaper here, the *Rheintaler*. Refugees were pouring into Switzerland from Czechoslovakia, but this time they were given a completely different reception by the government in Berne, of course. One day, when working with Dr Rohner's wife Gertrud (he was often in parliament in Berne), she was telling me about a situation in which she had been disappointed but where, she said, she would do the same thing again even if she knew the consequences in advance. That prompted me to say: 'Yes, that's what my father always says.' She then asked me to tell her exactly what had happened to my father as she had heard a few things but not the full story.

Her husband, to whom she later told the story, said the whole thing was scandalous and that something ought to be done. Above all, he said, something ought to be done to set the record straight and to let Switzerland know the true story of Paul Grueninger, because following my father's dismissal and trial all kinds of rumours had been spread about him and what he had done or was supposed to have done. Some people thought my father was fired for filching money from government accounts, others that he had accepted bribes from Jews. Soon after he was dismissed, Keel even went so far as to claim my father was psychologically ill and should be put into a psychiatric clinic – probably so that he could have said: 'This man is not normal' if my father had ever tried to lay some of the blame on him. A doctor was called and he put a stop to this insanity by saying that my father was absolutely normal and could not be interned in a clinic.

So without my father or anyone in his family really intending it, my father finally began to be recognised. Dr Rohner wrote an article for the local newspaper with the title: 'Injustice should be compensated', which set things in motion. The article was picked up by other newspapers in Switzerland and in Paris and in America. A Jewish US army general, Klein was his name, read about my father and he later came to St Gallen and met my parents and invited them to a reception in my father's honour. And then a film was made about my father by Felice Vitali.

It was also Dr Rohner who first asked the St Gallen government for the files to be reopened on the case, which after much hesitation they finally agreed to do. The government secretary at the time said there were hardly any documents left and that there was only one file. Dr Rohner was extremely busy, so his wife and I travelled to St Gallen a few times and went through what there was. And it was true there really was very little left. It had simply all disappeared, which is strange because my father often said that on many letters and other documents relating to the refugees he had written on the bottom: 'Approved by Regierungsrat Keel'. We did not find a single document or letter with this on.

Dr Rohner's goal was for my parents to be paid a small pension in their old age – they were pretty old by then – as a recognition of what my father had done for the Jews. But his efforts always ran up against the unwillingness of the authorities to agree to pay any financial compensation. The Social Democrats in the St Gallen government, who as a left-wing party you might have expected to be most likely to take up my father's cause, always resisted opening the case again because Regierungsrat Keel was a Social Democrat and they wanted to protect him. But after his death the Social Democrats seemed to become more interested in a rehabilitation.

In December 1970 my father finally received a letter from the St Gallen government recognising his contribution to helping Jews escape Nazi concentration camps, but this was not a real rehabilitation. The government said then, and it still says so now, that rehabilitation does not exist as an option under the law. But a rehabilitation would be meaningless now anyway. What use would a rehabilitation be to anyone now? It's all too late, really. It should have come much earlier. However, my father was still alive for the letter in 1970 from the government. At least he was alive for that, though it was shortly before his death. The letter pleased him very much. He had got used to the lack of money; if you have been forced to live for so many years with little money, you can become used to it.

My father was not bitter. He always said he had to act as he did and that he would have done the same again, even if he knew the consequences in advance. I find that really quite beautiful – if at the end one can say that, despite everything, one would do the same again. He was never really interested in seeing his name cleared or rehabilitated. He had had enough and wanted to be left alone. For me it has also been that way a bit. One does not always want to be reminded of the past.

He was a good-hearted man, not at all the stereotypical harsh policeman you might imagine. He helped many people: he was president of the St Gallen football club while he was still serving as a police commander, and was guarantor for a number of people who were in financial difficulties and indeed lost some money that way. But when he ran into difficulties no one stopped to help him. Some people broke off contact, they did not perhaps say it in so many words, but there were few people whom we could genuinely call our real friends – friends who stayed in touch after my father's dismissal. But it's always like that in life.

Today I would probably react differently, but then when it happened, when I was in Lausanne, I was too young and I didn't try very hard to help my father. But it was also a question of money and it would have needed a friend who was a lawyer to offer his services for free and that did not happen. We had relatives, of course, but most of them seemed to withdraw rather and few of them asked how we were doing or whether they could help. They were glad if we did not ask them for assistance.

In September 1971, just five months before he died, my father received a decoration from Israel in recognition of what he had done. That was very special for him. He was awarded something called the Medal of the Just, which is apparently rather unusual and presented to few people. The whole family was invited to Israel for a ceremony to receive the decoration, but my father was then 80 and was having some problems with his heart and his doctor advised him against making such a trip, because it might be too much for him. And so the ceremony was performed in Berne at the Israeli embassy. We were allowed to invite as many guests as we wanted to be present and so we asked Dr Rohner to come, my father's brother and a few others. Israel has also planted a number of trees in his honour and named a garden after him.

For Christmas that year he was given a present by the German president Gustav Heinemann. My grandmother had died and my parents had had to move out of her house because it was sold and they took a very small flat near where I was living with my husband in the village of Au. I just happened to look out of the balcony of my house one day and saw a big black car outside and some well-dressed men who were obviously looking for something. Then they went around the corner to the front door of my father's small house and rang the doorbell. I immediately went over to see my parents. Two officials from Bonn were there on behalf of the president and had come to ask if my parents had anything they wanted. We were all sitting in the very small lounge – the home was very modest – and the two men looked around and asked whether my parents had any particular wishes. My parents were also modest and replied: 'No, we have everything we need.' But the men pressed and asked if my parents wouldn't like to have a new sofa, but my parents said: 'No, no, we're quite happy with the one we have.' The two officials looked at each other and then they saw the black-and-white television and asked if my father wouldn't like to have a colour one and he waved the idea away. But I poked my elbow into my father's ribs and said: 'You like watching television so much and a colour television would be very nice for sports programmes, wouldn't it?' And then, at last, he agreed.

My father was someone who was prepared to accept what had happened and did not want to stir the whole thing up again. There was a lawyer in Zurich who had offered to open the case again, but my father was not interested. He simply thought that he had a clear conscience and that that was the most important thing. He regretted nothing.

Chronology

• The St Gallen cantonal government rejected calls for Grueninger's full legal rehabilitation – in effect a pardon – in 1968, 1969, 1970, 1984, 1989 and 1993.

- In 1970 the government sent Grueninger a letter recognising the humanity of his actions in 1938 and 1939. But it said it could not rehabilitate him because it would be very difficult to review all the circumstances that had led to the court's verdict at the time of the incident.

- Later, on 27 February 1985, the St Gallen government, in response to a further request in the cantonal parliament of St Gallen for the rehabilitation of Grueninger, said that it was legally impossible to rehabilitate Grueninger since such a process did not exist under cantonal law.

- On 30 November 1993, the St Gallen cantonal government declared it had decided on a political rehabilitation of Paul Grueninger. However, it said it would not be possible to give him a legal rehabilitation as this step was legally impossible and a reopening of the case after over 50 years, when most of the parties involved were no longer alive to give evidence, was not feasible.

- On 13 June 1994, the Swiss federal government commissioned an independent study to investigate whether a legal rehabilitation of Paul Grueninger was possible.

- On 30 November 1995 the St Gallen district court acquitted Paul Grueninger, posthumously, of all charges.

SWITZERLAND AND THE JEWS

Jacques Picard

Jacques Picard, a 42-year-old historian, studied history, literature
and economics at the universities of Berne and Fribourg. He spent
some time as a researcher in New York and is currently professor
of cultural history at an engineering school in Berne. His particular
interests are cultural history and the history of science and technology.

Picard has researched and published extensively on the history of
Jews in Switzerland. His most recent work is *Die Schweiz und
die Juden, 1933–1945*, a study of the troubled relationship between Switzerland and its Jewish community in this period. He
speaks in a dimly-lit attic room, which he uses for much of his
research, in the Obstberg quarter, near the old city centre of
Berne. Bookshelves line the walls.

The story of the Jews and Switzerland before and during the
Second World War is one of betrayal – the Swiss government mis-
led and betrayed their Jewish citizens, and in doing this it demon-
strated that anti-Semitic sentiment and attitudes were not far from
the surface in Swiss society. But let me start from the beginning.
It's important to know the history of relations between Switzerland
and its Jews to understand what happened in the 1930s and during
the Second World War.

Jews have lived in Switzerland for centuries, at least since the
official beginning of the Swiss confederation in 1291. However,
until the end of the nineteenth century they always had fewer rights

as citizens. This was, of course, little different from the rest of Europe, but in Switzerland the officially sanctioned discrimination continued for much longer than elsewhere and it required pressure from abroad before Swiss Jewish citizens finally won equality with other Swiss citizens.

As in most other European countries Swiss Jews in the Middle Ages were traditionally money-lenders because the Church forbade Christians to engage in this business. Towards the end of the fourteenth century, however, a number of Swiss towns began to ignore the Church's rules on money-lending by Christians. Over the century that followed this led to the expulsion of Jews from most Swiss towns. Jewish doctors were often allowed to stay longer, however, as they were much sought after for their medical knowledge – particularly during epidemics.

The Jews were subsequently allowed to live only in the *Untertanenlaender* (subordinate territories) of the confederation. These were areas that did not belong to the 13 core cantons of Switzerland but were on their fringes and under their control. Jews were tolerated in what is today Thurgau, the Rhine valley and the area around Baden. They settled in those Swiss towns where they could buy the protection of the authorities by paying a special tax. Jews were also charged the *Judengeleit* or *Judenzoll* (a duty) at many borders or bridges in Switzerland. By the late eighteenth century Swiss Jewry had concentrated in the two villages of Lengnau and Oberendingen, in the northern Swiss canton of Aargau. Here they were able to buy protection for themselves from the Grafschaft (county) of Baden and in Lengnau they built Switzerland's first Jewish synagogue in 1750. By 1850 some 1,500 Jews had settled in the two villages. However, although they were not persecuted, the discrimination continued. A Jew was forbidden from living in the same building as a Christian, could not own any property or land beyond his own house, and was not admitted into the guilds and thus excluded from all crafts. At first the Jews were not even allowed to bury their dead in Lengnau and Oberendingen, or anywhere else in Switzerland, but were forced to transport them to an island on the Rhine river on the border with Germany.

The French Revolution began the emancipation of Swiss Jews. The French government demanded that French Jews living in Switzerland be given the right to choose their place of residence, just as non-Jewish French citizens living in Switzerland could. France and Switzerland had signed a *Niederlassungsvertrag* (residency accord) which granted French and Swiss citizens mutual residency rights in each other's countries. The rights of French Jews living in Switzerland, although they were French citizens, were ignored by the Swiss. It was less the federal authorities than the cantonal governments, fearing an *Ueberjudung* (over-concentration of Jews), who bitterly resisted granting Jews the right to settle freely in the country. Foreign Jews and their governments, particularly in France, the Netherlands and the United States, criticised Switzerland's anti-Semitic laws. Indeed the United States provocatively appointed a Jewish ambassador to Berne. Finally, the Swiss government surrendered when the French government threatened to cancel the *Niederlassungsvertrag* unless the restrictions on French Jews in Switzerland were lifted.

But full legal emancipation for Swiss Jews took longer. The first federal constitution in 1848 did not give Jewish citizens all the rights that their Christian fellow citizens enjoyed. They could not choose where they wanted to live, were not equal to other citizens before the law, did not have the right to worship freely and could not vote. In 1856 the government agreed to enfranchise Jews, but only for local elections in their home cantons. It was not until the partial revision of the federal constitution in 1866 that Jews were also guaranteed the right to choose their place of residence and freedom of worship, and were regarded as equal before the law.

At the cantonal level anti-Semitic sentiment was much stronger. In Oberendingen and Lengnau a local emancipation law was passed in 1862; however, the law, which made the small villages into two political areas with equal rights to other Christian areas in the canton, could not be brought into effect until 1879 because of the strength of anti-Semitic feeling in the canton.

The *Niederlassungsvertrag* came back to haunt the Swiss government in the Second World War, when the question arose of how far Switzerland was prepared to protect its own Jewish citizens who were living in Vichy France. The Swiss foreign minister of the time, Marcel Pilet-Golaz, was asked in parliament by a Social Democratic parliamentarian in 1942 how Switzerland planned to protect the rights of these citizens. Pilet-Golaz answered that Swiss Jews abroad were subject to a different *ordre publique* from those living in Switzerland – in other words, Switzerland was abandoning them to their fate. The comment provoked a domestic political crisis. Swiss Jews accused the government of taking the first step on a slippery slope towards racial discrimination between Jewish citizens and other Swiss citizens. Of course, the reality was that Switzerland was helpless to protect Swiss Jews living in France.

Little did the Jewish community in Switzerland know then that their government had secretly already taken the first step on that slippery slope. In 1938 senior Swiss police officials in Berne, led by the chief of the federal police, Dr Heinrich Rothmund, began a series of secret negotiations with the German ambassador on how to stem the flow of German Jews into Switzerland. At the same time talks between the Swiss ambassador, Dr Hans Froelicher, and Nazi government officials also started in Berlin. The Swiss government feared it would be flooded with a wave of Jewish refugees that would lead to social tension and *Ueberfremdung* – loss of the national identity. This was hardly a genuine danger given the small numbers of Jews living in Switzerland; in 1930, for example, the number of Swiss and foreign Jews living in Switzerland represented around 0.4 or 0.5 per cent of the total population.

By the time the Swiss–German secret negotiations had started, the Nazis, following their 1936 Nuremberg Laws, were encouraging Jews to leave Germany and Austria. Once the Jews had crossed into Switzerland, the Nazi government would often refuse to take them back even if the Swiss authorities did not want to accept them. Switzerland was generally only willing to accept German Jews if they were in transit to other countries. However, other governments were becoming increasingly reluctant to take Jewish immigrants, leaving a rapidly growing number of Jews ostensibly in transit to other countries but, in effect, stuck in Switzerland. The Nazi Nuremberg Laws and the gradual deprivation of the Jews' civil rights in Germany and Austria in the late 1930s did not, in Swiss eyes, warrant classifying Jews leaving those two countries as political refugees.

The Swiss government threatened to introduce a visa requirement for all Germans entering the country unless the German government took steps to mark the passports of those citizens they were not prepared to accept back into Germany once they had left the country – in effect German Jews. For their part the Nazis desperately wanted to prevent the Swiss from introducing a visa requirement as they feared this would encourage other governments, on whom the Nazis also hoped to dump German Jews, to introduce the same measure.

In late 1938 the Nazi government eventually proposed marking all Jewish German passports with a red stamp on the first page. The stamp was a circle containing the letter 'J'; later it was just the 'J' without the circle. Swiss diplomats in Berlin readily agreed and were also in favour of meeting a Nazi demand that Switzerland reciprocate with the same distinguishing mark on Swiss Jewish passports so that German immigration officials could prevent them from entering Germany. Part of the reason that the Swiss embassy in Berlin could agree so easily to this discrimination of Swiss Jews was undoubtedly that they were witnessing at first hand the growing threat and danger Nazi Germany posed to the peace of Europe and were prepared to go to great lengths to maintain good relations between their two countries.

Rothmund refused outright to consider any reciprocal stamps on the passports of Swiss Jews. While accepting the 'J' stamp for German Jews as the best possible measure to control the Swiss border, Rothmund also expressed reservations about Swiss support for a measure that was directed solely at Jews and asked the Federal Council to take this into account when deciding whether to approve the policy. The Federal Council approved the measure on 4 October 1938.

Publicly the Swiss government only announced that it was introducing a visa requirement for non-Aryan Germans. But secretly it informed its consulates and embassies about the 'J' stamp and encouraged them to help the German government to enforce the measure as quickly as possible by sending German Jews, who requested entry into Switzerland, to the German authorities for the stamp first. The Swiss government was particularly worried about the consulates and embassies in Austria and Italy where many Swiss officials had been freely issuing visas to Austrian Jews they had taken pity on. The 'J' stamp was partly aimed at stopping German Jews at the border rather than catching them later on Swiss territory and trying to repatriate them by force to Germany – which was always a touchy domestic political issue. But the government, aiming to discipline the soft-hearted of its diplomats abroad, informed them confidentially that if necessary forced repatriations would be carried out. The Swiss–German negotiations on the 'J' stamp remained secret until the 1950s when the release of German documents first brought Swiss involvement in the policy to light.[1]

When Switzerland's contribution to the Holocaust became known after the Second World War the country's Jewish community justifiably felt it had been betrayed twice over. For, while secretly negotiating the 'J' stamp, the Swiss government had also forced Jewish charity groups and other Jewish organisations to foot the bill for those Jews who had managed to escape to Switzerland and were allowed to stay on condition that they were in transit or would return to their countries of origin once the situation there had normalised. It was made very clear to the Jewish community that the Swiss government would not pay for the refugees and that without the financial support of the Jewish community in Switzerland Berne would be forced to close its borders to the refugees. It should also be remembered that this was 1938, when the Nazi Nuremberg race laws were already three years old and when it was clear to every average, well-informed person that the Jews were being systematically deprived of their rights and persecuted in Germany.

From 1938 until 1944, by which time they had been squeezed dry, the Swiss Jews collected some 10 million Swiss francs to pay for the Jewish refugees from Germany, Austria and eastern Europe. They paid for their food, for their lodging and for their passage on to other countries. The fleeing Jews were powerless to provide for themselves since all refugees were forbidden from working as Swiss authorities did not want to generate unemployment. Ten million Swiss francs, of course, needs to be seen in relation to the value of money at the time. A loaf of bread, for example, then cost 44 centimes, compared with around three francs now. To give an idea of what kind of sacrifices the community of 18,000 Swiss Jews – of which only 5,000 were working and earning money – were required to make, had the whole Swiss population of 4.9 million at that time donated money in the same proportion then some three billion Swiss francs would have been collected, equivalent to around 18 billion francs today. Non-Jewish private charity organisations also contributed but not on the same scale and they also had to pay for the care of non-Jewish refugees arriving in Switzerland.

Support for the refugees stretched the financial resources of Swiss Jews to the limit and they were forced to look for support from Jewish communities abroad, particularly in the United States but also in South Africa, Canada, Australia – all places where large communities of Jews lived. Large amounts of Jewish money flowed into Switzerland immediately before and during the Second World War from Jews abroad. Switzerland, because of its geographical location, was the best escape route for Jews from Europe. The official Swiss policy that Jews only be allowed into Switzerland in transit was maintained until 1952, when the last Jewish refugee who had managed to escape the Nazis left Switzerland. In 1949, asylum and the right to stay in Switzerland was granted to refugees over 52 years of age. Again the authorities had been careful to ensure the refugees would not destabilise the local labour market and also would not represent a racial danger.

During the War the government tightened border controls considerably to guard against an influx of refugees from the conflict zone. All foreigners now required visas, regardless of whether they were in transit or not. After the outbreak of the War in Europe in 1939 any foreigners entering Switzerland illegally could be expelled and returned to their country of origin, with the exception of deserters from foreign armies and those classified as political refugees.

In early August 1942, with the flow of refugees to Switzerland growing rapidly and the government terrified of an uncontrollable inundation, border controls were tightened further, restricting entry for foreigners even if it was suspected they were facing considerable personal danger and risks in the countries from which they were fleeing. Less than two weeks later, on 13 August, police chief Rothmund instructed all border posts to refuse entry to all civilian refugees, an instruction that was rigorously carried out. This, however, provoked sharp criticism not only from Swiss Jews but from the Swiss population in general and in parliament. The Federal Council and Rothmund were forced to ease these restrictions on 25 August.

It was now that Justice Minister Eduard von Steiger made his famous speech to the *Junge Kirche* (Young Church) in Zurich on 30 August, in which he justified a tough Swiss policy on refugees using the metaphor of the lifeboat that was already full. By September border controls had tightened again as Rothmund's department issued instructions reaffirming that racial grounds were insufficient to warrant classification as a political refugee and that French Jews in particular must not be allowed into the country under any circumstances, as they did not face any dangers or risks in France. In October the Swiss army then sealed the border completely, posting troops on the frontier and erecting barbed wire fences. Foreigners, including Jews, arriving at the border were turned back and some who managed to cross illegally were dragged back over the frontier. The federal police, however, accepted a list of names from Swiss church groups of prominent people suffering persecution in Germany or German-occupied territories and agreed to allow them into the country if they showed up at the Swiss frontier. The numbers of political refugees granted entry into Switzerland fell sharply once the borders were sealed. In September just under 4,000 foreigners had been granted refuge; after the borders were closed this number halved.

It was not until the tide of the War had clearly turned against the Nazis and domestic criticism had reached a peak that the Swiss government finally had the courage to change its policies. In October 1943 Switzerland opened its borders and began to take in refugees again. Following the collapse of Italy and its occupation by German forces Switzerland started allowing civilian refugees, including Jews, from the conflict into the country. But it was not until July 1944 that the police department formally lifted the instruction to its border posts that racial refugees were not political refugees. Now the Swiss government actively tried to help save Jews and offered to take 14,000 Hungarian Jews after Nazi forces occupied Hungary and began rounding up Jews for extermination. However, few of these Jews actually ever reached Switzerland.

From 1943 the government also began to offer both Jewish and non-Jewish refugees some financial support, in the form of work camps where men were put to physical labour and women to work washing and weaving. In return for their labour they were provided with room and board. Previously refugees without means had mostly been living in barracks funded by private charities. Just as it had left the support of Jewish refugees to Jewish organisations, the Swiss government had required other charities and refugee organisations in Switzerland to meet the bills for non-Jewish refugees.

We will never know exactly how many Jews were turned back at the Swiss border or forced back over the border if they were arrested after entering the country illegally. We will also not know how many Jews decided against even trying to escape to Switzerland because of the policies of the Swiss government. But figures delivered to the federal police by border posts during the War show that from August 1942, when Berne first began hermetically sealing the country's frontiers, to the end of the War just under 10,000 people were turned back by the border police. Since Switzerland readily gave refuge to foreign military personnel fleeing conflict throughout the War, these 10,000 must have been civilian refugees and it is safe to assume that a fair number were Jews.[2]

So we have a situation in which the Swiss government entered into a tacit agreement with its Jewish citizens that if they paid for their brethren fleeing the Nazis then the Swiss government would not stop them entering the country. But at the same time the government broke this agreement by secretly cooperating with the German government's racial discrimination against German Jews; then in 1942, when the genocide reached its height with the Final Solution in Germany, the door was slammed shut on all Jewish refugees.

One must always remember, however, when criticising the Swiss government that Switzerland was under enormous external pressure. In the late 1930s and until 1942 nobody knew whether Switzerland would be the next victim of the Nazi *blitzkrieg* machine. Berne was desperate to avoid provoking a Nazi invasion. The Swiss Jews were under the same pressure and similarly did not want themselves or their refugees to be the catalyst for such an invasion. Many Jews emigrated. In 1938 taxes paid by Jews in the city of Zurich fell by one-third. Those who could afford it – the upper middle class and the wealthy – left the country.

But, despite the pressures, there was a clear anti-Semitic, racial undertone to the Swiss government's policy. Apart from anything else this was evident from the way other refugees were treated by the Swiss authorities. Non-Jewish refugees were not classified into Catholic or Protestant categories and the Swiss Catholic or Protestant communities were not expected to pay for their respective refugees. Thus while other refugees were financed by refugee charities in general, the Swiss government in effect relegated the Jews to the status of second-grade refugees and told the Jewish community to sort out and pay for its own refugee problem. If Berne had demanded all charities participate in the financing for Jewish refugees – the charities that are part of the *Schweizerische Fluechtlingshilfe* (Swiss Refugee Assistance) – the policy would have been acceptable. But to demand Swiss Jews foot the bill for their refugees, while other refugees, regardless of religion, were funded by charitable organisations in general is a racial distinction and morally questionable.

Notes

1. The negotiations between Switzerland and Germany that led to the 'J' stamp only became public in 1954 when the United States published German foreign ministry documents which revealed that Switzerland had played a role in this discrimination. This triggered domestic political outrage, but Swiss Jews were very circumspect and reacted very cautiously. This was the same generation that had lived through the Second World War and that had learnt to survive by having as low a political profile as possible. During and before the War Swiss Jews had cooperated with Berne, being careful to perform their patriotic duties. When they discovered after the War that the government had secretly betrayed them, the experience was painful; but they remained careful in their public criticism. Following the revelations the government ordered an investigation which led to the *Ludwig Report* of 1959 by the Basle professor Carl Ludwig. The report issued no moral verdict but simply came to the conclusion that the period before and during the Second World War had been difficult and that Switzerland had also done things it did not deserve to be proud of.

2. During the Second World War Switzerland was a refuge for 295,000 foreigners. Most of them were military personnel who, in line with international conventions, were financed and supplied by their home countries. There were around 50,000 civilian refugees; in addition 60,000 children were evacuated to Switzerland by the Red Cross and there were also short-term border refugees who may have entered Switzerland purely to escape military conflicts on the other side of the border. Between 1933 and 1952 some 29,500 Jews entered Switzerland.

Chronology

- 27 October 1891: Paul Grueninger born in St Gallen.
- 1919: Grueninger joins police force as lieutenant.
- 1925: Grueninger promoted to captain (Hauptmann).
- 28 March 1938: Swiss federal council introduces visa requirement for Austrian citizens following flood of Jewish immigrants from Austria after *Anschluss* with Germany and first pogroms against Jews in Austria.
- April 1938: Swiss federal police and embassy in Berlin begin negotiations with German authorities on marking of German Jewish passports. Leads to agreement on 'J' stamp.
- 10 August 1938: Federal police for foreigners reports to justice ministry that 1,000 illegal immigrants are now in Switzerland and that unless illegal entry

is stopped there is a danger of a situation developing which the country would be unable to cope with.

- 12 August 1938: *Israelitische Fluechtlingshilfe* announces that over 200 illegal Jewish refugees had arrived from Austria and were without means.
- 14 August 1938: Camp set up at Diepoldsau on Swiss–Austrian border for Jewish refugees. Further camps in canton of St Gallen.
- 18 August 1938: Swiss justice ministry rules that all Austrians without a visa must be barred from entering Switzerland.
- 19 August 1938: Swiss Federal Council approves justice ministry's decision and determines that all Austrian refugees without a visa must without exception be sent back to Austria or be sent on to other countries. *Israelitische Fluechtlingshilfe* reports well over 400 illegal Jewish refugees.
- 4 October 1938: Swiss Federal Council approves a secret agreement with Germany under which all German Jews have their passports stamped with a 'J'. Publicly Swiss government says it is introducing a visa requirement for non-Aryan Germans.
- 24 November 1938: *Neue Zuercher Zeitung* publishes article entitled 'Murder of all the Jews in Germany?'. Article reprinted by *St Gallen Volkstimme*.
- 6–7 January 1939: Chief of foreign police in the justice ministry holds talks with Regierungsrat Valentin Keel and demands an investigation of the high refugee numbers in St Gallen.
- 20 January 1939: Swiss federal government introduces visa requirement for all foreign refugees.
- 26 January 1939: Grueninger presents Keel with 'adjusted' figures on refugees.
- 11 February 1939: Rothmund letter to Keel again demands an investigation.
- 20 February 1939: Rothmund says there are 10,000 to 12,000 refugees in Switzerland of which some 3,000 are Jews without means.
- Mid-February 1939: Gustav Studer, head of St Gallen cantonal foreign police, starts the investigation of Grueninger.
- 13 March 1939: Sidney Dreifuss, textile agent and head of the *Israelitische Fluechtlingshilfe* in St Gallen, admits to falsifying records on refugee numbers and says he followed instructions from Grueninger.
- 27 March 1939: St Gallen government council, after receipt of Gustav Studer's report, decides on an administrative investigation of Grueninger.
- 31 March 1939: St Gallen government council decides to suspend Grueninger and starts a criminal investigation.
- 12 May 1939: St Gallen cantonal government council decides on immediate dismissal of Paul Grueninger.
- 5 September 1939: Swiss federal government decides on a visa requirement for all foreigners, including those in transit.
- 17 October 1939: Swiss federal government rules that all foreigners entering Switzerland illegally be expelled to their country of origin immediately. Deserters and those classified as political refugees are the only exceptions. Jews are not considered to be political refugees.
- 1 October 1940: Public trial of Grueninger in St Gallen communal court.

- 23 December 1940: Second hearing for Grueninger in St Gallen communal court.
- 14 March 1941: Written verdict and sentence sent to Grueninger. Grueninger does not appeal.
- 13 August 1942: Rothmund orders border police to refuse entry to all civilian refugees.
- 24 August 1942: Justice Minister Eduard von Steiger orders Rothmund measures be eased.
- 9 October 1942: Swiss army seals Switzerland's borders with France and Germany, setting up barbed wire fences.
- 12 July 1944: Swiss federal police give border police new instructions on refugees. The ruling that refugees fleeing racial persecution are not to be considered political refugees is dropped.
- 3 November 1944: Rothmund protests to German authorities about Jewish deportations and says Switzerland is willing to take German Jews as refugees.
- 1953: Grueninger receives 300 Swiss francs from the World Jewish Congress.
- October 1969: Grueninger receives 1,000 Swiss francs with letter of congratulation on his birthday from the *Schweizerische Israelitische Gemeinschaftsbund* (Swiss Federation of Jewish Communities). (SIG was founded in 1904 to fight for Jewish rights and against anti-Semitic prejudice in Switzerland. During the 1930s it had to counter the right-wing *Fronten-Fruehling* political movement in Switzerland which called for restriction of Jewish civil rights.)
- September 1971: Grueninger awarded Medal of the Just by Israeli museum and research institute Yad Vashem in Jerusalem.
- Christmas 1971: Grueninger presented with colour television by German President, Gustav Heinemann.
- 22 February 1972: Grueninger's death.

Chapter 2

SWITZERLAND AND THE BANKS

If you see a Swiss banker jump out of the window, jump after him. There's bound to be money in it.[1]

Swiss banks have as ambiguous a reputation today as they had for Voltaire in the eighteenth century. They conjure up images of numbered accounts, secretive financial transactions and bankers who will do business with anyone, criminal or otherwise, as long as the price is right. Unfair and misleading cry the bankers: the anonymous numbered accounts no longer exist; the secrecy has been curtailed; and the banks no longer want your business if you are on the wrong side of the law.

Yet millions of dollars extorted by disreputable current or former dictators around the world, profits generated from the international drug trade and massive bribe payments continue to surface in Swiss bank accounts.[2] Swiss banks are estimated to manage a massive 1,200 billion Swiss francs and critics intimate that not all of this is legal money. Nevertheless, the bankers continue to protest their innocence, saying that Swiss legislation against money laundering is now among the toughest in the world and that criminals would be foolish to try and launder their money in Switzerland. But in the same breath they warn that money launderers have become more sophisticated and that it is impossible to guarantee all the money on their books is 'clean'.

The crux of the problem is banking secrecy – the bankers' professional code of confidentiality that has been codified in Swiss law since 1934. The discretion of Swiss banks, that this law both allowed and required, has attracted many unsavoury customers and often obstructed their prosecution. Ironically the banking secrecy, that is abused by criminals today, was introduced in Switzerland with the best of intentions. The 1934 law prevented bankers releasing information on their German Jewish clients to the Third Reich. But after the Second World War the very same law bound the bankers to resist pressure from Jewish refugee groups and the Swiss authorities for information on the accounts of Holocaust victims. The question of whether Swiss banks still hold money that belonged to Jews killed under the Nazi regime of persecution remains unanswered.

In this chapter Jacques Picard describes the battle between the banks and Jewish groups over the Holocaust money. Picard is one of the very few historians who has researched Swiss government archives to discover the fate of funds deposited in Switzerland before and during the Second World War by the racially, religiously and politically persecuted.

Paul Rechsteiner, a lawyer and a member of parliament for the Social Democratic Party, criticises Swiss banks for opportunistically hiding behind banking secrecy while profiting handsomely from the money of tax dodgers and criminals.

Robert Studer, head of Switzerland's largest bank and among the most respected and influential of Swiss bankers, speaks on both of these subjects from the banker's point of view. He also discusses management philosophy and the relationship between military and business leadership.

Notes

1. The eighteenth-century French philosopher Voltaire, quoted on the frontispiece of Jean Ziegler (1982).

2. In one of the most recent cases – and the country's largest ever – Union Bank of Switzerland announced in April 1994 that it had suspended one of its fund managers who was under suspicion of having managed for the last 15 years an account worth $132 million which Swiss authorities suspected originated from international drug dealing. Swiss media reported at the time that the money was believed to belong to a Colombian group related to the notorious Medellin drug cartel.

HOLOCAUST MONEY AND SWISS BANKS

Jacques Picard

As part of his work on the history of Jews in Switzerland Jacques Picard has also investigated the fate of the Holocaust money. He has written an unpublished study on how in the 50 years since the Second World War the Swiss authorities, banks and Jewish groups have tried to resolve the question (Picard, 1993). However, the issue was never settled to the satisfaction of all parties involved and still remains emotionally charged. Picard argues that the amount of Holocaust money officially declared by banks and other organisations in Switzerland was suspiciously low. He says that if the banks are interested in clearing the suspicions that remain over the issue they should allow historians access to internal minutes and records.

Imagine the situation. It is Nazi Germany, and a Jewish father who knows he and his family are going to be arrested and thrown into a concentration camp wonders what to do with the bank documents on his accounts in Switzerland, accounts to which he has carefully transferred his hard-earned savings a few years earlier when the Nazis started depriving Jews of their civil rights. He might hide the documents, but equally he might burn them, saying to his 15-year-old son: 'We have an account in Switzerland. This is the name of the bank. If anything happens to me or your mother, the money is there.'

Ten years later the parents are dead – victims of the Holocaust – and the son, who feels it is a miracle that he is alive at all, emigrates to Israel and forgets all about the bank account. But perhaps he does not forget; he does remember that his father mentioned an account, but he probably does not remember the name of the bank, the account number his father gave him, or the pseudonym under which the father had registered the account to ensure its secrecy. And even if he remembers all the details he may not have any papers that enable him to prove either his identity or that he is the son of the account holder.

Even without the Nazi persecution Jews would probably not have kept many bank documents or records because many were breaking local currency regulations or capital export regulations of the countries in which they were living when they deposited funds in Swiss banks. The money did not only come from Jews in Germany, but also from Jews in other countries conquered by the Germans. It also came from non-Jews who may have had something to fear from the Nazis. But whatever the origin of the funds, the account holders would have been very careful not to keep many potentially incriminating bank documents as the Nazi persecution worsened.

Wealthy Jews could have confidence that Swiss banks were a safe haven because of the 1934 banking secrecy law which is really the key to the whole issue of unclaimed funds. There was a tradition of hiding money in Swiss banks that stretched back at least as far as the time of the French Revolution, when French aristocrats had brought their valuables to private banks in Geneva for safekeeping. But the banking secrecy law ensured the banks were that much safer because it made it legal for banks to keep information on their customers and clients secret. The law was passed partly because Swiss banks and the government wanted to ensure totalitarian regimes in Europe would not be able to get their hands on money held abroad by citizens they disapproved of. In the case of Germany the law reassured Jews that their capital would be safe from the prying eyes of the Nazi regime. In the 1930s the Swiss federal court, which is the highest court in Switzerland, rejected a number of appeals by the Nazi government to force Swiss banks to release information on the capital of German Jews held in Switzerland. This only further encouraged Jews to entrust their funds to Swiss banks, and also to lawyers, notaries and other trust or fund managers in Switzerland.

Some of that money is undoubtedly still in Swiss banks or with the trusts, fund managers or insurance companies it was deposited with. Neither the banks, nor anyone else, knows to whom the money now belongs. This does not apply only to Swiss banks but also to British, Swedish and American banks which also took on a lot of Jewish money and were also restricted by banking secrecy laws after the Second World War. It is difficult to judge without accurate information, but Switzerland was probably one of the more important countries for this kind of Jewish flight capital, because of its political stability and because of its status and tradition as a neutral country.

After the Second World War the very same banking secrecy law which had protected the wealth of the persecuted so well, suddenly became a problem for Switzerland and a *bête noire* for the Jewish community. The Allied countries, mainly Britain and the United States, put pressure on Switzerland to hand over German assets held in Swiss banks as German reparations for the War. It was not only a question of the wealth of German citizens but also of bullion from the Nazi Reichsbank.[1] For the Swiss there was no more justification for releasing German capital to the Allies than there had been for providing the Nazis with access to Jewish funds held in Switzerland. However, the United States had quite a lot of leverage over Switzerland because it had frozen some 4.3 billion Swiss francs' worth of assets belonging to Swiss companies in the United States in 1941. Under the Enemy Act the Americans had blocked all assets belonging to continental European countries. As far as Jewish assets in Switzerland were concerned, the Allies demanded the Swiss government give any money belonging to victims of the Holocaust to Jewish charity organisations. Britain and the United States had themselves come under some pressure on this issue. In 1947 the International Refugee Organisation (IRO) had called on the major powers to negotiate with neutral countries such as Switzerland over the release of unclaimed funds. In the case of Switzerland the IRO said that banking secrecy would have to be lifted. However, with the exception of the Reichsbank gold, the Swiss managed to wriggle out of the Allied demands, keeping most German assets in Switzerland and agreeing only to consider the question of donating unclaimed money from Nazi victims to charity.

But this was not the end of the story. Jewish groups in Switzerland and abroad wanted the question of the unclaimed funds of victims of the Holocaust settled. The *Schweizerische Israelitische*

Gemeindebund (SIG) (Swiss Federation of Jewish Communities)[2] and the Jewish World Congress met Swiss government representatives in 1946 for initial discussions. In 1947 the SIG issued a report which listed a few cases which it said were just the tip of the iceberg. One example was a Swiss shoe company which had a number of Jewish representatives abroad. These representatives had disappeared, but there were still 75 bank accounts in their names in Swiss banks. Another example was a property worth two million Swiss francs that was being managed by a major Swiss bank because the fate of the Jewish owner was unknown.

The Swiss government, that is the justice ministry, was finally forced to act and organised three separate inquiries in 1947, 1949 and 1956 in which it asked Swiss banks and insurance companies how much money they had on their books which they suspected was unclaimed Jewish money. They were told to look for capital belonging to clients with Jewish-sounding names and where there had been no communication with the clients since 1945. The results of the three inquiries varied but totals of such funds ranged between 200,000 and 800,000 Swiss francs. Then in a report of its own in 1957 the justice ministry said the unclaimed Jewish money in Switzerland probably totalled under one million Swiss francs. However, it warned that there might still be other unclaimed Jewish valuables and assets in safe deposit boxes, either rented for long periods and therefore not yet opened by the banks, or perhaps administered by lawyers or friends of the victims. Since the amount of money that was eventually declared was ten times the ministry's estimate it seems the banks, lawyers, insurers and so on were, at this stage, not making as rigorous a search through their books as they did later.

In the meantime the Swiss Bankers' Association and the SIG, who were really the two adversaries in the issue, had been meeting face to face between 1952 and 1954 to try and find a way of solving the problem. The SIG argued that the Holocaust was an exceptional situation, in which not only individuals but entire extended families across several generations had been exterminated, that meant there were no immediately apparent heirs for many unclaimed assets. It said the problem could only be solved if the Swiss banking secrecy law was suspended so that distant heirs could be found for the unclaimed capital, or, if there were no heirs, the money could be donated to charities.

For the bankers banking secrecy was sacrosanct and they did not want it touched. They said any such step should be postponed for at least 20 or 30 years until the situation had clarified itself. The bankers stated that they had already tried very hard to identify unclaimed funds immediately after the War, and warned that they had been flooded with letters and inquiries after 1945 – many of which had clearly been sent speculatively by charlatans and opportunists. Furthermore, they said, Switzerland was not the only country where Jewish money had been hidden. Banks in the United States had also taken in huge sums. Finally, they claimed, many of the funds had already been reclaimed by the legitimate owners or their heirs. The banks also insisted that the amounts of money involved were much lower than SIG suspected.

The problem was not an easy one for the banks to deal with. The majority of bankers, notaries, lawyers and fund managers were probably honest and upright citizens who genuinely wanted to do their utmost to ensure the unclaimed assets were returned to their rightful heirs. And they undoubtedly did investigate the fate of their clients and their heirs as far as was possible. But even if the intentions were good the bankers and lawyers were constrained by their code of conduct. They could not simply make a public appeal for information on the whereabouts of Mr X without making it public that Mr X was a client of theirs and thus exposing themselves, should Mr X ever show up, to charges of breaching banking secrecy. For the same reason, even discreet inquiries among known friends of their clients would have been risky.

Of course, there were also black sheep in the financial services community and all sides either openly or tacitly acknowledged this. But without completely dismembering the laws on banking and lawyers' secrecy it was impossible to know whether bankers, insurers and lawyers were deliberately taking advantage of the Holocaust and enriching themselves – simply not making any effort to find the heirs and hoping that with time the money would simply become theirs – or actually trying, in a confidential manner, to find the legitimate owners.

The matter was further complicated by the Cold War. Many clients or legitimate heirs were behind the Iron Curtain and there was a danger that if the assets were returned to them they would simply be confiscated by the communist governments involved. The Polish and Hungarian governments had already approached the

Swiss government on this issue soon after the Second World War and had demanded the return not only of assets belonging to Polish individuals and companies but also of Polish assets stolen by the Nazis and deposited in Switzerland. The SIG argued furiously against this. Returning the funds to these countries would be equivalent to nationalising them and might even cause political difficulties for the owners or their heirs.

The parliamentary discussions over what to do about the problem began in the late 1950s and continued until December 1962. The law that was finally passed in December 1962 was a compromise that pleased neither the banks nor the lawyers. It partly lifted banking and lawyers' secrecy and confidentiality. It gave anyone who was holding money, jewellery and valuables in safe deposit boxes or any other assets that they suspected might have belonged to Jews, or any other racially, religiously or politically persecuted people and who had not had any information on the whereabouts of these people since the end of the Second World War, ten years to declare the amounts involved to the authorities. These authorities would then try and find the owners or their heirs. If after two years no owners or heirs had been found, the money involved was to be placed in a fund that would be administered by the government. Anyone found to be giving false information or not cooperating was liable to punishment; however, there was no system of control or supervision to check how rigorously the banks and other organisations were adhering to the law. Such a system would have required a full lifting of banking secrecy, allowing independent auditors to look through the books of the banks – a situation the bankers would not have countenanced.

The law also recognised the danger of putting clients or heirs in Eastern Europe at risk. It forbade searching for heirs if there was a real risk of causing difficulties for the people being sought – in other words, people in Eastern Europe. Swiss inheritance law was also changed for the same reason. Previously under inheritance law the state was entitled to all money of Swiss citizens for which there were no heirs. This would have meant that foreign states would have been entitled to claim heirless funds which had belonged to their citizens and were held in Switzerland. The revision prevented this.

The government appointed Heinz Häberlin, a former director of a cantonal bank in Thurgau, to run the office responsible for unearthing owners and heirs of the money that was declared by banks and other organisations and individuals. However, he was only responsible for those searches that the local authorities in Switzerland felt unable to undertake on their own. The larger cities made their own inquiries. In western Europe Häberlin used a German group called *Internationaler Suchdienst* (International Search Service). For potential owners or heirs behind the Iron Curtain he contacted the international Red Cross and also used private Jewish channels. Häberlin dealt with 698 cases, of which 325 involved less than 500 Swiss francs each. In 132 cases – worth a total 1.67 million Swiss francs – the owners or heirs were found, mostly in the United States and Israel. In 228 cases the assets remained unclaimed and were put in the government's fund. A further 151 of Häberlin's cases concerned people either living or believed to be living behind the Iron Curtain.

The total amount of money and valuables that was finally declared was, in my opinion, very little – indeed, suspiciously little – amounting to 9.47 million Swiss francs. The banks had declared 6.07 million Swiss francs; the Swiss *Verrechnungsstelle*, which includes the post office and the central bank, 2.47 million; local authorities, fund managers and private individuals 670,000 Swiss francs; and insurance companies around 260,000 Swiss francs. The government said that some 7,000 requests for the return of assets had been received and processed but that almost all were rejected as illegitimate. About three-quarters of the declared money was returned to its owners or their heirs. The remainder went into the government's fund which was then divided, with two-thirds going to the SIG and one-third to the Swiss Refugee Assistance organisation.[3]

My instinctive feeling is that banks, particularly large banks, had little to gain from concealing such money and everything to gain from handing it out to its rightful owners. This could only improve their image domestically and abroad. But we do not know how carefully they went through their books looking for Jewish assets. And the fact remains that the amount of money declared seems very, very little.

Lawyers, however, were in a different situation because they do not need to project a pristine public image as the large banks do. A lawyer could be honest, but he might also be 'forgetful'; alternatively he might simply be criminal. The lawyers reported the least amount of Holocaust money between 1962 and 1972.

To find out whether there is more money in the banks than was declared one would need to have access to internal bank archives, and the minutes of meetings of the executive management where discussions were held and decisions taken on how rigorously to look for Holocaust money. If the banks are interested in a full historical clarification of the issue then they should open their records and archives. If they have nothing to hide then their records will only support their claims that there is no such money left.

[*Author's note*: Finally, it must also be noted that it is not only the fate of Holocaust money that remains shrouded in mystery. In 1994 a former employee of a major Swiss bank was found guilty by a Zurich court of fraud and falsification of documents after having transferred some 134,000 Swiss francs from the account of a deceased customer of the bank to the account of an accomplice in 1991. The affair came to light when the son and heir of the deceased inquired at the bank in early 1994 about his father's deposits. A representative of the bank admitted to a reporter of the *Neue Zurecher Zeitung*[4] at the trial that if the deceased customer had not had any heirs the illegal transfer would probably never have been discovered.]

Notes

1. Under Allied pressure Switzerland agreed in 1946 to hand over some 51 tonnes of gold which it had bought from Nazi Germany's Reichsbank during the War but which was part of a stock of nearly 200 tonnes of gold belonging to the Belgian central bank. To show the transfer was made under protest, the president of the Swiss National Bank refused to sign the final document authorising this transfer, arguing that the Swiss had bought the gold in good faith and had no means of knowing what its origin was. The gold had been entrusted to the Bank of France by the Belgian national bank before the Nazi invasion of Belgium. Following the German occupation of France the French Vichy government capitulated to Nazi demands and transferred the gold that had been hidden in Senegal to the Reichsbank. It has never been clarified whether some of the gold that a number of central banks bought from the Reichsbank during the War (the Nazis sold the gold to meet their foreign exchange needs) was gold that the Reichsbank had melted into ingots from the gold fillings and jewellery of Jewish Holocaust victims. (For more details, see Gian Trepp, 1993.) US intelligence documents declassified in 1996 quote a Nazi German economics ministry official telling US interrogators after the Second World War in 1946 that Nazi Germany had transferred 15 billion

Reichmarks (equivalent to some $6 billion in 1945) in assets to Switzerland between 1939 and 1945 (Reuters news service, 7 June 1996).

2. The SIG was founded in 1904 to fight for Jewish rights and against anti-Semitic prejudice in Switzerland. During the 1930s it had had to counter the right-wing *Fronten-Fruehling* political movement in Switzerland which had demanded Jewish civil rights be restricted.

3. The SIG passed its share of the money on to the American Jewish Joint Distribution Committee, a relief and social welfare organisation which had provided financial support for Jewish refugees during the War.

4. *Neue Zuercher Zeitung*, Saturday 3/4 September 1994.

SWITZERLAND AND CAPITAL FLIGHT

Paul Rechsteiner

Paul Rechsteiner, 42 years old, has been a Social Democratic Party
member of the lower house of parliament (Nationalrat) since 1986.
He presided over a Social Democratic parliamentary party committee investigating the role of Swiss banks in the Italian corruption scandals. He is also a member of the *Erklaerung von Bern*
(EvB).[1] In private life he is a lawyer in the north-eastern university
town of St Gallen, where he was also born and grew up. Rechsteiner studied law in Fribourg and Berlin. He is particularly
interested in legal cases involving labour law and socio-political
issues. He spoke at a small table covered with books and papers
in his office. A computer hummed intermittently in the background
and his secretary clattered at a typewriter in the next room.

Where do you start when it comes to capital flight? How do you
define it? On one level we are talking about tax evasion. Any time
large sums of capital are deposited in a Swiss bank account you
just have to assume from the word 'go' that the money is at least
evading tax or currency regulations in the country it has come
from. So one definition of capital flight is money or capital that is
exported illegally and transferred to other countries where it can
be hidden or is out of the reach of the authorities in the country
of origin.

A second kind of capital flight is money which is exported from
a country because the owners of the money do not like the particular political or economic system of that country. What happens
is that the rich classes export the wealth of the country and deprive

the country, its economy and its people of capital which could be
used to help the country develop. It is exploitation because the
capital is no longer available to the country. It is perhaps acceptable
for the honest worker in the Third World, who has managed to
build up some savings, to want to secure these against inflation
and to invest these outside the unstable country in which he or she
lives. But we are not talking about these comparatively small
amounts of money; we are talking about huge sums owned by the
'super-rich' which could be invested in the economy and which are
vital to the development of a country.

Here the banks argue that this kind of capital export is legitimate because it preserves the value and purchasing power of the
capital. But this is not acceptable. It is simply an attempt to take a
value-free approach to the whole problem and to see the money
that is fleeing foreign countries as legitimate investments by those
seeking protection against inflation and loss of value. Bankers
simply ignore the fact that much of this money has been accumu-
lated illegally. It is not a question of a value-free economic process,
but of a process that demonstrates the exploitation that is going
on in these countries – an exploitation that leads to the poverty in
which large sections of the population in these countries live. It is,
in reality, a matter of robbery and not of value-free accounting
processes. It is a moral issue.

The third kind of capital flight is the worst – capital flight in its
most evil form. It is the export of the massive fortunes of the
political élite such as dictators like Mobutu[2] and Marcos,[3] leaders
who are often the criminals responsible for the poverty and deprivation of their countries and their people. By agreeing to manage
this booty Swiss banks give these criminals a kind of insurance in
protecting against financial insecurity should they suddenly have
to flee their countries. In a legal sense you can try and argue that
this is not stolen money because local laws have not been broken,
although often they have. But in a moral sense the money is stolen.
The billions that Mobutu has stashed in banks in the West may
have been amassed legally according to Zairean law, but in both
an economic and moral sense it is daylight robbery. Even if the
political system in the country does not prevent a ruler from ex-
ploiting the country for personal ends, often through the use of
force, it is still morally wrong.

Of course, the question of how much Third World capital flight money is hoarded in Swiss banks is very difficult – in fact impossible – to answer. This is because of the secrecy of the banks and also because Switzerland does not publish the necessary statistics on capital imports. The *Erklaerung von Bern* often uses a 1986 study by McKinsey on Swiss private banks which estimated that these handle some 250 to 300 billion Swiss francs from the Third World.[4] Most of that money almost certainly falls into one of the three categories of capital flight mentioned above.

The weakness of Swiss laws in this area and the government's lack of interest in stopping capital flight make Swiss banks very attractive to foreigners wanting to hide their money abroad. There has so far only been one case where the Swiss government has, on its own initiative, ignored banking secrecy and the powerful banking lobby and taken a moral position on the side of the exploited, and that is in the case of the Marcos fortune. Immediately following the fall of Marcos in the Philippines in 1986 the *Bundesrat* (Federal Council) froze all Marcos money in Swiss banks to ensure it was not withdrawn and concealed elsewhere. The Swiss were also giving the new Philippine government time to gather evidence on the money Marcos had siphoned out of the country and to bring criminal charges against him. Criminal charges also have to be brought in Switzerland, for crimes that are illegal under Swiss law, before Swiss courts will waive banking secrecy and offer judicial assistance. Judicial assistance means a Swiss court orders a bank to give access to confidential documents with details on the ownership of accounts, and payments in and out of the accounts. The Philippines, however, was reluctant to try Marcos because of the political risk of allowing him back into the country following his exile. After Marcos's death the Philippine authorities brought charges against his widow and some documents on the Marcos accounts have now been released. However, even in this case where Switzerland has cooperated by freezing the funds, the money remains in Swiss banks and will only be released if Imelda Marcos is found guilty. And even then the return of the money is not guaranteed because a direct link between the crime she is found guilty of and the money in the banks has to be proved.

The Marcos case was an exception. Clearly in the *Bundesrat* at the time there was a majority, if not a consensus, that the reputation of Switzerland would have suffered too much if the Swiss had simply washed their hands of the whole business and not undertaken some measure in solidarity with the Aquino[5] government. The decision was an emergency one, however, because under normal Swiss legal procedures it would not have been possible to freeze the money in that manner. There was undoubtedly also pressure from the United States and from world public opinion in general and it was widely known, or at least suspected, that a significant proportion of the Marcos money was in Swiss bank accounts.

But although the case of the Marcos money shows Switzerland can undertake measures to stop immoral capital flight if it wants to, it unfortunately also shows how the combination of Swiss banking secrecy and the ineffectiveness of Switzerland's judicial assistance make it almost impossible to return the money. Switzerland says it is prepared to cooperate internationally with the authorities of other countries, but the possibilities for cooperation are so limited that, in the end, the interests of the people hoarding their money in Swiss banks are still served best.

The 'hot' capital flight issue of the moment is the Italian political corruption scandal. I am the head of a Social Democratic Party parliamentary committee investigating this whole issue. It is clear that considerable sums of bribery money were paid into Swiss bank accounts – indeed the payment into Swiss bank accounts was commonly the chosen method of concealing the bribes. But the Swiss authorities are helpless and the judicial assistance they can give Italian prosecutors is close to zero because, under Swiss law, bribery in a foreign country is not a crime.[6] So once again the money remains in the banks and those who have broken the law come off best.

The Italian case simply shows once more that Swiss banking secrecy functions so well because of the weakness of Switzerland's laws on judicial assistance. Money in Swiss bank accounts from bribery in a foreign country is part of the first category of capital flight, together with tax evasion and evasion of exchange controls. Under current Swiss law it is also impossible to extend judicial assistance to governments investigating breaches of currency or tax regulations in their countries. All this kind of money is 'grey money' and the corrupt and the tax evaders around the world are benefiting from the weakness of Swiss laws.

So the question is: how can Switzerland put a stop to this ridiculous situation in which Swiss law, in effect, protects criminals and their ill-gotten gains? If Switzerland seriously wanted to deal with this problem then it would have to change Swiss law so that better judicial assistance could be offered to foreign governments. At the moment Swiss banking secrecy and Swiss law often make it difficult for foreign governments to gather evidence against criminals in their own countries.

If judicial assistance was more flexible and banking secrecy less rigid, it would be easy to make a clear distinction between funds flowing into Swiss banks that are genuine and legal and those which are illegal capital flight. And Switzerland would also be helping those countries suffering from the effects of capital flight. There are some things happening in this area and the *Bundesrat* has promised to present a proposal that would speed up the process for judicial assistance. However, even these proposals will not change the fact that breaches of currency regulations and tax evasion abroad are not crimes warranting Swiss judicial assistance. And without judicial assistance for investigations into all this 'grey money', little will change and this form of capital flight will continue unrestricted.

The crucial problem is how to get banks to inform the authorities when they believe they have illegal money on their books. Currently there is a lot of discussion about the right (*Melderecht*) and the duty (*Meldepflicht*)[7] of bankers to report suspected criminal money to the authorities. But these will always be meaningless as long as there is no recognition of tax evasion and evasion of currency regulations as crimes warranting Swiss judicial assistance.

Melderecht and *Meldepflicht* are not irrelevant, but they do not have the central significance that they are often presented as having. It becomes very difficult to make clear distinctions between criminal money and legal money if Swiss law does not classify 'grey money' as illegal and if Swiss banks actually want this kind of money. It only becomes possible to distinguish between criminal and legal money when the distinction is very crass and obvious, such as in the case of the Marcos fortune. In the majority of cases it is impossible to draw clear-cut, black-and-white distinctions and this means Swiss regulations have a purely symbolic nature.

What would also help to deal with the problem is greater transparency of bank accounts, and this is something that the *Erklaerung von Bern* and the Social Democratic Party have been demanding for a long time. With more transparency it would be easier to hold a more factual and less unpleasant, ideological debate over what role Swiss banks play in capital flight. People do not like to talk about capital flight very much here. The discretion of the Swiss is not just one of the main attractions for foreigners depositing money here, it also serves a useful purpose for the national conscience, allowing a suppression of the problem to avoid feeling guilty about it. It tarnishes the view the Swiss have of themselves – of a country which, through honest hard work, developed in a few generations from a poor country without raw materials to one of the richest countries on earth. The Swiss do not really want to know the dirty details of how this has happened and what the reasons are for this wealth.

These legal changes would help control capital flight, but I know, of course, that the chances of introducing these reforms are very slight. The banks have very strong lobbies and a lot of political influence in Switzerland and, since they have no interest in supporting any significant change to the situation, it is very difficult to bring about reform.

Reform would perhaps be possible if the United States put greater pressure on Switzerland. Whenever the United States has done this, things have changed comparatively quickly here, for example in the case of legislation against insider trading. It was made clear to Swiss banks by the American authorities that they would face great difficulties winning US approval for the opening of branches or subsidiaries in the United States unless Switzerland made insider trading illegal, in order that it could then offer judicial assistance in insider trading cases to US authorities. There is now a law in Switzerland forbidding insider dealing. Unfortunately for the Third World it does not have the necessary economic and political clout to be able to pressure Switzerland into passing legislation against capital flight in this way.

The reforms I am talking about have also become more unlikely since the vote against membership of the European Economic Area in 1992.[8] Since then the political right wing in parliament has gained strength, and the desire and interest of the centre and left-wing parties to press for further laws and again to risk confrontation with the right wing has flagged. At most there is a willingness to pass symbolic legislation.

Unfortunately the will to take this step, to remove these loopholes where Switzerland does not offer judicial assistance, is not very strong here. There is a long tradition of criticism of the banks in Switzerland and in particular of criticism of this particular role or activity of the banks, but this criticism has always remained a minority view. The Social Democratic Party collected enough signatures to force a referendum on this issue, among other things, after the Chiasso Scandal of 1977.[9] In the referendum the party wanted to improve judicial assistance as a sign of solidarity with Third World countries. It also wanted laws requiring the banks to lift banking secrecy in order to control tax evasion and for them to provide information on their hidden reserves. The referendum was finally held in the mid-1980s but failed miserably, not coming anywhere near to getting the necessary majority. There have always been forces in Switzerland – and not solely from within the banking lobby – that have fought to preserve banking secrecy, and these forces remain very strong. It is part of the political climate here.

Some argue that Switzerland would be unnecessarily shooting itself in the foot by driving the grey money away and that the whole economy would suffer. But the question is really whether it is in Switzerland's long-term interest to remain a haven for flight capital and for all kinds of grey and black money. Ultimately, it is a question of what kind of view of the future one has for Switzerland. I am not convinced that a future as some kind of pirates' lair is preferable to the development into a country that is prepared to take on its duties and responsibilities in the international world community. But in order to fulfil its responsibilities to the wider community, Switzerland must support those fighting crime and not offer efficient services to criminals.

Notes

1. The *Erklaerung von Bern* (EvB) is one of the leading organisations in Switzerland critical of Swiss banks for accepting flight capital from the Third World. It was founded in 1968 with a manifesto, signed by over 10,000 Swiss citizens, calling for fairer relations with the Third World. Currently the EvB has some 18,000 members. It is a non-governmental, independent organisation that finances itself through membership fees and the sale of its publications. The EvB also criticises drug dumping in the Third World by Swiss pharmaceutical companies. It demands a balanced relationship between North and South in nutritional matters and opposes the export of seed derived from gene technology which it says would make the South even more dependent on the multinationals of the North. It was opposed to Swiss membership of the

International Monetary Fund, which it said sucked more capital out of the Third World than it lent to it. However, despite this opposition Swiss voters in 1992 approved Switzerland's membership of the World Bank and the IMF.

2. Zaire's President Mobutu is believed to have amassed a fortune of several billion dollars, much of which, it is claimed, is stored in Swiss banks or in Swiss property. The Swiss government has so far rejected calls for these assets to be frozen.

3. The Philippine government has since 1986 been trying to get its hands on money and gold said to have been plundered from the Philippines and hoarded in Swiss banks by its former president, Ferdinand Marcos. Estimates of the total amount of Marcos assets in Swiss banks range from hundreds of millions to billions of Swiss francs. Persistent rumours over several years that gold bullion belonging to the Marcos family was stored at a bonded warehouse at Zurich airport finally led to a search of the premises by a Zurich district prosecutor in early 1994. No gold was found. Some $350 million have been frozen by Swiss authorities since Marcos was toppled in 1986. The highest Swiss court has ruled that the money cannot be handed over to the Philippine government until it has been proven in a fair trial that the accounts contain the proceeds of criminal activities, that is, activities which are illegal under Swiss law. To establish this the Manila government in 1993 brought over 90 criminal and civil charges against Imelda Marcos, Ferdinand Marcos's widow, accusing her of plundering the Philippine Treasury. The Philippine government claims Marcos funds in Switzerland could total $3.5 billion.

4. Estimates of Third World capital flight vary widely and are very difficult to make. EvB says the total capital flight from the Third World to Switzerland and other countries is around 1,000 billion Swiss francs. It cites a 1986 study on the private banking market by McKinsey and Company in Switzerland that estimated on the basis of interviews with private bankers that Swiss banks managed some 250 to 300 billion Swiss francs' worth of funds from Third World countries (McKinsey and Company, 1986).

In contrast a former economist at Crédit Suisse, a major Swiss bank, estimated in a 1990 publication that some $12 to $19 billion of capital fled from the Third World between 1974 and 1985 (Mast, 1990).

5. Corazon Aquino came to power as the first President of the Philippines after the peaceful revolution against Ferdinand Marcos.

6. The Financial Action Task Force, a 16-member group set up in 1989 which now includes Switzerland, makes recommendations to governments on how to stop money laundering. The FATF is currently working on a recommended code of behaviour for member countries that would bind governments to waive banking secrecy in order to help prosecute cases of corruption in other countries.

7. The Swiss parliament passed legislation in early 1994 giving bankers and financiers the right to report suspicious client transactions to authorities without infringing banking secrecy laws. The so-called *Melderecht* (right to

report) frees the banker from the legal obligation of confidentiality if a client is believed to be depositing illegal money in the bank. The law also makes membership of a criminal organisation a punishable offence in an attempt to stop money launderers hiding behind legal 'shell' companies and forcing Swiss authorities into making much more exhaustive and difficult searches to ascertain whether the money in question originates from criminal activity. Under the new law the court assumes the money is 'dirty' if the owner is a member of a criminal organisation and the onus is on the accused to prove the money is 'clean'.

In June 1996 the government approved a draft law that would turn the *Melderecht* into a *Meldepflicht* – an obligation to report suspicions to authorities. An extension of the banks' due diligence obligations to cover companies or individuals offering financial services has also been suggested. (For details, see note 2 in the following interview: The Swiss Banker.)

The government has also promised a fourth package of measures aimed at speeding up judicial assistance for foreign governments investigating money laundering in their own countries and needing information from Swiss financial organisations.

8. The Swiss electorate voted narrowly against joining the European Economic Area, a giant market including the member states of the European Union and the European Free Trade Area, in December 1992.

9. In the 1977 Chiasso scandal the southern Swiss Chiasso branch of Crédit Suisse, one of Switzerland's three largest banks, was found to be involved in the illegal export of billions of Swiss francs' worth of capital from Italy for wealthy clients there who feared the Communist Party would win sufficient votes in the impending general election to force the ruling Christian Democrats into a coalition government. The illegal transfers were discovered and exposed by the authorities. The management of the Chiasso branch of Crédit Suisse was charged, tried and sentenced to gaol terms. The director of the branch, Erich Kuhrmeier, was found dead in his cell two months after he was imprisoned. He had suffered a heart attack. Crédit Suisse suffered financial losses of 2.5 billion Swiss francs.

THE SWISS BANKER

Robert Studer

Robert Studer, 56 years old, is chief executive of Switzerland's largest bank. A personally shy man, who never speaks publicly about his private life, Studer's youthful appearance, athletic build and disarming manner do not match the clichéd image of one of Switzerland's most powerful bankers. Studer speaks in his third-floor office of the bank's headquarters on Zurich's Bahnhofstrasse. Hanging on the wall behind him is a steel plaque with the inscription: 'Lead, Follow Or Get Out Of The Way'. Occasionally he repeats a phrase he has just said, steeples his hands and ruminates over what to say next. When he talks his eyes search for contact with his interlocutor.

This issue of so-called unclaimed Jewish money in Swiss banks rears its head again and again. For us it is no issue at all. The problem was thoroughly discussed after the Second World War and we conscientiously investigated then what money in our bank might have belonged to Holocaust victims because we wanted to settle the question once and for all. For us the case is closed.

I think people often underestimate the ability of those who are under pressure or in difficulties to organise themselves, despite the difficulties. It has almost always been the case that people have found some way of informing somebody about their money. Otherwise they would not have been able and would not have had the initiative to open an account in the first place during those difficult times before and during the Second World War. They did not open an account just by themselves and alone without telling anyone, particularly with the risks in Germany at the time of them disappearing without trace and without anyone knowing about their accounts. The account they opened and the money they deposited was organised via lawyers.

Before and during the Second World War Swiss banks allowed their clients unrestricted right of proxy and this meant there never really was a problem with unclaimed funds after the War. A customer could give power of proxy to a lawyer or to any person – it did not matter who. All the representative of the customer needed to do was give his or her signature and they had access to the accounts, and after the War the owners or their heirs would have got their money from these representatives. They were well organised and the power of proxy ensured there was very little unclaimed money washing around the banks after the War. Here I have no problem with my conscience.

If anyone was to question me about how much money there is in our bank that is not owned by somebody, I would answer that there is no such money.

We did a lot of work in this area. We had to be very careful because some people turned up and were claiming horrendously large sums – that, of course, happens in these sorts of situations – and I think part of the myth that huge sums of Jewish money were lying unclaimed in Swiss banks comes from this time when vast and completely exaggerated and unrealistic sums of money were claimed, some of it even by official organisations. This is the same phenomenon as those huge demands for compensation one often sees being made under civil law, when someone makes an initial demand that is very high because they expect to have to compromise at a much lower level.

We have never considered opening our bank archives to allow historians to research how the banks went about checking their books for this kind of money. We have the longest storage period for documents in the whole world and if we opened the archives I think it would only be after 50 years. I'm sure, however, that the archives from the 1960s, when the banks were checking their books for any money belonging to Holocaust victims, still exist. However, in short, we do not believe there is any problem with unclaimed Jewish money in Swiss banks.[1]

We certainly take seriously the criticism that Swiss banks do not do enough to stop capital flight from the Third World and other countries to accounts here in Switzerland. However, you need to be careful before you criticise Swiss banks for this. The large sums of private money from Italy, France, Mexico and other countries that are accepted by Swiss banks are often funds that are fleeing political and economic risk in those countries. If a country – such as France over the last 30 years – switches between applying strict controls on foreign exchange transactions and capital transfers and removing them, that is that country's business and it is not our job to play politics. It is similarly the case if money is exported from high-inflation countries. I know of no capital, whether it is being transferred to Switzerland, London, America or Germany, that comes from countries where there is political stability and where the devaluation of money is at a low level. Capital flight only occurs from countries that are politically unstable and where money devaluation is high. And you see it again and again that as soon as political stability is re-established the capital returns.

This leads to the question of whether, in fact, this sort of capital flight does not make a lot of economic sense since it enables people to maintain the purchasing power of their money or at least to reduce the erosion of its purchasing power. I see it in this bank. Quite a large proportion of our foreign customers are not particularly interested in whether their capital grows or not, they simply want the purchasing power of their capital to be maintained. You can see this from the fact that despite the boom cycle we have been having on share markets, over two-thirds of our customers have chosen to remain in fixed-rate investments. People want to preserve the purchasing power of their capital. One sees this very clearly in the case of Italy: as soon as inflation falls and there is a measure of political and economic stability, the money returns.

Is this bad? Are Swiss banks doing something wrong in providing this kind of service? I have no problem with this. I take the criticism seriously, but I think it is unjustified. I am convinced that rather than have the state take the money from the wealthy through devaluation or exaggerated taxation or whatever, it is better for all concerned, including the lower social classes in these countries, that the economy is stabilized and the flight capital is attracted back to the country. This is precisely what is happening in Mexico now and in Argentina – the money is returning in large amounts. If the money no longer existed because it had all been lost to devaluation, economic recovery would not be possible. On this issue I also have no problem with my conscience.

As far as the laundering of criminal money through Swiss banks is concerned, we undertake everything possible to block corrupt capital or criminal money in general from flowing into our accounts. We certainly don't want that kind of money. It makes no sense in business terms because sooner or later it becomes public if we are holding such money and then it harms our reputation so badly that it damages our business. Of course it is sometimes difficult to determine what is criminal money and there are shell companies or front men everywhere. But the bottom line is very clear: we do not want criminal money.

I am sure that Switzerland has some of the toughest measures and defences against money laundering of any financial centre in the world. What the European Union has introduced, but only as a recommendation,[2] has been binding in Switzerland since 1977.[3] In this area we are far ahead of the rest of the world. But we need to remain on our guard, because criminals use new and increasingly sophisticated tricks. The daytime robberies on the Bahnhofstrasse here in Zurich when handbags are seized did not occur a few years ago. If criminals start riding bicycles along the street and grab your bag as they pass you then they are using a new technique, a new trick. Similarly criminals are always developing new ways of hiding money. We always assume a client is honest. But sometimes it is difficult to discover the truth, of course. We don't accept all money that is brought to us without question. The client must identify himself or herself.

However, I am sure that despite our most strenuous efforts, which include regular training courses and so on, we undoubtedly have criminal money in this bank. After all, it is a well-known characteristic of money that, sooner or later, it ends up in a bank. As far as countering money laundering is concerned, Switzerland is very far advanced and if I had to launder money I would avoid Switzerland.

[*Author's note*: Union Bank of Switzerland is widely regarded as the 'military bank' in Switzerland, the bank where a successful military career does most to further a man's career in the bank. When asked about this Studer smiles.]

I am always amused by the widespread opinion or claim that a military career helps a career in the bank and that without military connections you have no hope of reaching the top in this bank. If I look at my colleagues on the executive board it is obvious that this is not true: Mr Cabbiallavetta is a private; Mr Janjoeri is a private or a lance-corporal; Mr Heckmann is a colonel; Mr Grete a colonel; I am a colonel; and Mr de Weck is, I think, a private.

For me the question of the link between the military career and the civilian career is really the question of leadership. It is difficult to find people who are prepared to take responsibility for leadership, it is difficult to find people who are prepared to stand up in the public eye and defend our position and what we do. The subject is not the army, but the ability to perform a difficult leadership role and I think that today the people who can fulfil that role have even better chances than I have had. When I was around 21 years old and serving as a lieutenant I gave orders and the soldiers obeyed. As a lieutenant in today's army I would have to deal with twenty to twenty-five men, many of whom do not want to do military service, and who think the whole business stinks, and who question not only military service but the sense of having an army at all. I think the leadership tasks that one has to carry out today are much more difficult than they were twenty to thirty years ago and therefore the leadership experience is a much better one than it was then.

Where else do you have the opportunity at the age of 20 or 21 to lead twenty or so people of your own age who do not want to be commanded but from whom you must win respect if you are to get them to obey you effectively? Who else gives you this opportunity? No one. If you go to Harvard you do case study after case study. To carry out a project you do an analysis of the situation, formulate an outlook for what you want to achieve and then decide how this can be achieved. This is the training you will get from every business management school. And this training is also relevant. Here in the bank I can call on the advice of experts, I can set up working parties and then, finally, I reach a decision.

But now the difficulty arises: I don't know if our employees will support the decision and I have to persuade them, I don't know if the competition has in the meantime developed a better plan on the same subject, I don't know how clients will react, I don't know how the markets will react, and so on. The execution of a decision is not something you can learn in a management school. You can go through case studies, but you can never experience what it is like to be 'under fire' other than in the army.

If I ask myself where we have the greatest problem at the

moment then the answer is in the leadership of people. That is our major management problem – the leadership of people. And the problem starts with the people who join the bank at the bottom. How should they be inducted into the bank? It's the same problem in every company. The most resignations happen in the first year, because new employees are not inducted properly. The leadership of people is decisive, it is the main problem that we have. And I am of the opinion that this problem is at its greatest where we have people in leadership positions who have had little or no chance to gain practical experience in leading people.

Many in Switzerland understandably argue that we can no longer afford to have people away for months on end in the army. They argue that learning leadership for five weeks a year in these difficult and competitive times is simply too expensive. I fully understand this view, but I believe it is wrong in the long term. I think if we were to give up, or greatly reduce this opportunity for learning how to lead people, then in ten to twenty years the quality of leadership would decline sharply throughout the country and reverberate throughout the economy.

People say to me that the military is a place where you give orders and a soldier has to obey whether he likes it or not. But that is not the case. Today you cannot simply give orders and expect them to be carried out and obeyed. It is the same in business – only when you have persuaded subordinates can you expect them to follow you. There have been only two undertakings over the centuries from which we can and should learn something about leadership structures: one is the Church and the other is the army. And I think one should study and benefit from these experiences.

But one needs to understand what leadership in the army means. It means in practice that I tell you where we want to go, but how you get there is left up to you. And that is the principle we try to pursue in the bank. So if, for example, you were the chief executive for East Asia and we told you our objectives and what the available resources were, you would have to decide how you would realise those objectives and then tell us your intentions. That's how we operate. And that is how all successful armies of the world operate – with this freedom and independence. The job for General Schwarzkopf was very simple; the resources were UN troops and the job was to free Kuwait. Operation Desert Storm exemplified military leadership at its best. The best military leadership is delegation. That was not done in Vietnam, where President Johnson and McNamara[4] determined which buildings should be bombed in North Vietnam. That is not how military leadership works. The military orders should have been: liberate North Vietnam. These are the resources. This is the time frame. George Bush was a president who understood what military leadership means; Johnson was not.

The plaque on my wall here – 'Lead, Follow Or Get Out Of The Way' – is to be understood in that way. Either people are prepared to take the responsibility for leadership and also the risk of making mistakes, or they are not. Only those who do not want the responsibility of leadership can be sure they will not make mistakes. If they don't want responsibility and want to avoid making mistakes then they must be prepared to receive orders and carry them out. People who are not willing to do either cannot be used.

Notes

1. Studer told a news conference in February 1996, however, that UBS had found 10.5 million Swiss francs in accounts in the bank following an investigation prompted by pressure from the World Jewish Congress which claimed in 1995 that Swiss banks were hoarding billions of dollars in unclaimed assets of Holocaust victims. The pressure from the World Jewish Congress led the Swiss Banking Association to order an investigation of Swiss banks to search for dormant accounts. The Association said in February 1996 that it had unearthed a total of $34 million in Swiss financial institutions of unclaimed assets, possibly belonging to the heirs of Holocaust victims (Reuters News Service, 23 February 1996). In May the Swiss Bankers' Association agreed to set up an independent international panel with international Jewish groups to look for Holocaust accounts in Swiss banks.

2. A 1991 EC directive, 91/308/EEC, required banks and other credit institutions to identify their clients and to keep records for five years after an account is closed. In cases when 15,000 European Currency Units or more is deposited or moved as a single transaction or series of transactions, the bank must know who the client is or who controls an account opened by proxy. The measures were due to take effect throughout the European Union from 1993 but by the end of the year only France, Luxembourg and Italy had enacted the directive into national legislation.

3. In 1977 Swiss banks and the Swiss Bankers' Association signed an Agreement on the Rules of Due Diligence (*Vereinbarung ueber die Standesregeln ueber die Sorgfaltspflicht*). The agreement, which lays down rules of business

conduct for Swiss banks, was in reaction to the 1977 Chiasso scandal (see note 9 in the previous section: Switzerland and Capital Flight) and has since been revised three times – in 1982, 1987 and 1992. The current version of the agreement forbids active assistance by banks to capital flight and requires banks to identify clients in cash transactions involving more than 25,000 Swiss francs. Infringements can lead to fines of up to 10 million francs (see Schweizer Bankier Vereinigung, 1991/92). However, the agreement is criticised for not stopping banks from passively accepting illegal money. In August 1990 Switzerland outlawed money laundering. This law punishes those who undertake actions which conceal the origin and prevent the confiscation of money earned through criminal activity.

4. Robert S. McNamara was US Secretary of Defense from 1960 to 1967 during the administrations of Presidents John F. Kennedy and Lyndon B. Johnson.

Chapter 3

THE ZURICH DRUG PROBLEM: FROM NEEDLE PARK TO LETTENSTEG

He saw the notebook and immediately came up to ask what I was writing. He swayed a little when standing but said he felt relatively good because he had just had his shot for the day. 'Do you want to ask me questions? I can help you.' The crooks of both his arms and his forearms were pockmarked with needle marks. He had a tube of vein-softening cream, which one of the volunteers at the syringe distribution window had given to him, and was massaging the cream into his face. 'It's to stop the veins going hard from all the drugs, but I use it to keep the skin of my face soft.' We walked through a throng of dealers calling out the drugs they had to sell and addicts preparing mixtures of heroin, cocaine and methadone. A man tied the leash of his dog to a fence, knelt down in front of the wing mirror of a parked car and felt for a vein in his neck in which to inject a full syringe.

We sat down on a low stone wall on the river bank. He looked young, barely out of adolescence. 'I am 21 years old. I have been coming here for nearly four years.' He had moved to Switzerland with his parents from Yugoslavia when he was a young child. Later his parents divorced. 'I had a girlfriend and one day she said she wanted to try taking drugs.' Occasionally he runs his fingers through his wavy black hair. Unlike most of those around him his clothes are clean and he looks as if he washes regularly. He is sweating, although it is not hot, probably because the mixture he has pumped into his veins is beginning to take hold of his body. 'I tried to stop her, but she wouldn't. We argued a lot and then one day I tried it as well. That was four years ago.' His girlfriend has disappeared now. 'I don't know where she is. She disappeared two years ago. I hope she comes back.'

He finances the drugs by prostituting himself to men he meets in the public toilets in Zurich central train station which is just across the street, barely a stone's throw from where we are sitting. 'That usually gets me a couple of hundred francs which is enough for my daily fix. But if I don't get the money then it's difficult.'

He says he is fortunate because he has a place to live. 'I share a flat with a man, he's older than me. He lets me stay there and

gives me clothes and food as long as I do certain things for him.'
The distribution of sterile syringes is very useful, he says,
gesturing at the large open window of the small hut where addicts
are given a sterile syringe for every used one they throw into a
blood-spattered vat. Condoms, sterile wipes and fresh water are
all available. He does not think about AIDS. 'It is much better
here since they started the syringe exchange service.'

He looks up suddenly at a short, pot-bellied man who has
materialised in front of us. 'I am not ready yet, you will have to
wait. Can't you see I am busy?' he says in annoyance. The short
man sits down on the wall next to us. The young man continues,
but the atmosphere has been irretrievably disturbed and he is no
longer talking freely. A little later the short man gets up impatiently.
They exchange a few sharp words and then he gets up as well.
'Thank you very much for the conversation.' We shake hands and
they walk away together.

Platzspitz, October 1990

Zurich, Switzerland's largest city, had the largest open drug scene
in Europe in the early 1990s. Platzspitz, a park in central Zurich,
was closed in early 1992 and the scene shifted a couple of hundred metres along the Limmat river to an old disused railway
siding called Lettensteg. In 1995 Lettensteg was closed down by
city authorities and the drug scene dispersed into the city's back
streets, thus coming full circle back to a policy that existed in the
1980s in Zurich. In 1995 359 addicts died of drug-related causes
in Switzerland as a whole, a large part of those in Zurich. According to official statistics there are an estimated 12,000 to 24,000
HIV+ people in Switzerland. By the end of April 1994, 3,747 cases
of Acquired Immune Deficiency Syndrome (AIDS) had been registered in Switzerland. Of these 2,637 had already died. Close to a
half of all the recorded AIDS cases were drug addicts.

In this chapter three individuals, all of whom have devoted many
years of their lives to helping drug addicts in Zurich and elsewhere
in Switzerland, offer three alternative approaches to dealing with
the problem.

Former city councillor Emilie Lieberherr, who has been involved
in the Zurich drug problem from the beginning, argues for the
legalisation of drug consumption and medically-supervised dis-

tribution of drugs by the state. Only in this way, she feels, will the evil of drug dealers and the international drug trade be destroyed. Father Ernst Sieber, a member of parliament, runs a network of centres for the homeless, alcoholics and drug addicts. His solution is for addicts to live in kibbutz-like villages where the support of a close-knit community would give individuals the strength to break their addiction. Werner Fuchs, a leading medical specialist on drug addiction who has worked on radical projects to combat the spread of AIDS among addicts, says Swiss society must accept that drug addiction is as much a part of everyday life as alcoholism and must abandon the idea that there is a way of eradicating the problem.

THE POLITICIAN

Emilie Lieberherr

Emilie Lieberherr, at 69 years old, is a tall, large woman who has the energy of someone half her age. She talks in her office, volubly and gesticulating, usually leaning back in her chair but occasionally stretching forward to stress a point. The interview is a few weeks before her retirement from the Zurich city government council where she has served without interruption for 24 years. In 1970 Lieberherr was the first woman to be elected to the council, almost immediately after women were given the vote in the canton of Zurich.[1]

Known for her strong and unconventional views, Lieberherr is also the only member of the city council standing on an independent political platform. In 1982 she was dropped from the Social Democratic Party's list of candidates for the council elections and in 1990 expelled from the party. 'The break between me and the Social Democratic Party had nothing to do with my drug policy – the party is less advanced on drugs than I am. No, it was apparently because I had made the unforgivable mistake of supporting someone for the city presidency who was not the approved Social Democratic candidate.'

Lieberherr describes herself as a very political person. 'I lived through the 1930s as a schoolgirl, but I was a politically-conscious schoolgirl. Maybe that surprises you, maybe it doesn't. I did not live in Zurich, and I was born in the Urschweiz (one of the founding cantons of Switzerland). I come from a family where there was a lot of discussion. I went to a convent school and there was also a lot of discussion there because we had a lot of foreign schoolgirls from families who had fled Nazi Germany. I am very, very sensitive when it comes to the infringement of human rights, particularly of drug addicts.'

Lieberherr is looking forward to retirement. 'Once I step down from the city council I won't fade away as some of my enemies are probably hoping. I will still be active. I will be involved in three areas. One is drug policy, the second is old-age policy – I have been elected president of the largest pensioners' association in Switzerland – and the third is unemployment issues.

I have been involved in the Zurich drug problem ever since drugs became a political issue in this city. Drugs really started as a political problem after the police closed down the *Autonomes Jugend Zentrum* (Autonomous Youth Centre). This was at the time of the youth disturbances in 1980 involving radical left-wing groups. Of course we had drugs before that. We had quite heavy drug consumption during the 1968 student movement just as there was among students throughout the Western world who were all following the trend from America. But it was not until the youth movement and the disturbances of 1980 that drugs began to become a political issue, in both Zurich and Switzerland in general, and a problem that everyone started worrying about.

The AJZ was meant to be a totally autonomous centre for the youth movement, free of all bourgeois, conventional, capitalist influences. And drugs were part of this alternative lifestyle so the AJZ also wanted to set up a room for people shooting up. They did not want any help from the government or the authorities, they wanted to remain totally autonomous. No police or any representatives of authority or social workers were to be allowed in. But they did want government money and a place, a building for their AJZ. And they got both.

The dispute I had with those people at the time was over how one best deals with people needing social assistance. When the AJZ centre opened I said to them: 'Be careful you don't attract too many social welfare problem cases!' But they did not listen. They always said they could deal with these cases better than professional social workers. They wanted to show that with their new lifestyle, based on solidarity with each other, fewer social problems arise and those that do can be better solved. I offered them help. I said they could have ten social workers to help, but they refused the offer. They only wanted money. And so the city parliament decided that I should give them government money. Six months later they reappeared and said they needed the social

workers I had offered them after all. They even said I should have
forced them to accept the social workers earlier! What could I say?
I told them they were adults and responsible for their own actions,
that I was not their mother and that it was too late.

But political sentiment in Zurich was changing. The bourgeois
parties were gaining the upper hand and elections in Zurich were
due. The city government decided to close down the AJZ. The
drug addicts who had been using the rooms there found themselves
on the street and from that point on we had an open drug scene in
Zurich. Since then we have had this absurd situation of the police
trying to chase the addicts off the streets and the addicts simply
moving to another location whenever the police close down the
existing one.

After the AJZ was closed the addicts congregated on the shore
of Lake Zurich for a while, then when the police harassment became too much they moved to Bahnhof Stadelhofen just next to
the opera house – and so on around the city until they finally
landed in Platzspitz.[2] This was by now the late 1980s, and both
the city government and the parliament decided to tolerate the
existence of the open drug scene at Platzspitz as long as it was
contained within the park. It became famous abroad in the newspapers and on television as 'Needle Park'.

But by 1991 Platzspitz had become unacceptable. It was acting
as a magnet for drug addicts from all over Switzerland and even
from the rest of Europe. And that, of course, attracted many drug
dealers. Soon foreign drug dealers, most of them here illegally or
posing as refugees seeking political asylum, had control of the
market. The battle for market share became aggressive and more
and more people at Platzspitz started carrying weapons. Almost
inevitably there were fights, and people were killed.

In the city council we could see that the situation was deterior-
ating rapidly and so we asked our drug team to compile a report
on Platzspitz in the summer of 1991. The report advised that
Platzspitz should be closed, but recommended that before it was
shut down alternative facilities should be set up for the addicts. I
had already started talking with the heads of local communal
councils outside the city in the canton of Zurich about alternative
facilities when the Statthalter (delegate of the cantonal government)
ordered the closure of Platzspitz in January 1992. His order came
just two weeks before national parliamentary elections, elections

in which he was a candidate for the conservative *Christliche Volks-partei* (Christian People's Party).

We held a meeting in the city council and a majority of us decided to accept the order. I hurriedly strengthened and expanded what facilities we already had outside Platzspitz. But I also gave a very clear warning that closing Platzspitz would not solve the problem, and we would simply go back to the old cat-and-mouse game between the police and the addicts. And that is exactly what has happened. The drug scene simply flooded into the nearby Industrie-quartier (a predominantly working-class area of Zurich called the industry quarter). It was certainly a mistake to close Platzspitz at that particular moment and at such short notice.

Now the open drug scene has moved to Lettensteg and the conditions there for the addicts are much worse than they were at Platzspitz. It is beneath human dignity to gather on an old railway siding. The chasing around by the police is also much worse than before; not long ago the police said they would take a tougher line, but it has not made any difference to the number of addicts. I was down at Lettensteg not long ago. The addicts had already heard that I was going to stand down from the city council this year and it was very moving to see how worried they were about the future. They held on to me and asked: 'Who will look after us when you are gone?' I feel very strongly for these people when they talk to me openly, when they tell me what is happening to them, and when they show me their wounds.

On the one hand I could cry that in a wealthy society like Zurich – where just one kilometre away from the Lettensteg there are billions of francs in the banks, where there is great luxury and people who can afford so many things – we also have these people who have no future and who have been through terrible experiences. I don't ask if it is their fault or not. Just as I don't ask an alcoholic: 'Why are you drinking, why are you so weak, why can't you get away from the bottle?' On the other hand I feel a fury – a fury that we have so much stubbornness and so many people who believe that you can solve the drug problem simply by getting rid of these people with repression. I always get angry when I see the police chasing people on the streets simply because they have orders to prevent people gathering at a particular spot. I always get a little sharp with the police when I see that and ask them if they have nothing better to do than chase poor, helpless people around.

It makes me furious that people, even colleagues of mine in the city council, agree not only with this repression but believe that by chasing helpless addicts around the streets one can solve the problem.

The Zurich drug problem is different from the problems in other cities in Europe because it is open – out on the streets. I have seen the different kinds of drug problems experienced in all major European cities; I am involved in the Frankfurt Resolution.[3] Many cities in Europe have a drug problem but we are the only city with a large, open drug scene.

My major opponent in the city council was the councillor for the health office and he favours repression as a drug policy. Unfortunately this repression also meant an end to the ZIPP-AIDS project,[4] which was doing a lot of very good work, in 1992. The city government supported the project for three years, from 1989 to 1992. But after the closure of Platzspitz and the start of the new regime of repression, the project was seen as one of the reasons addicts were drawn to Zurich from all over the country. I am afraid that with all this chasing about the streets and without ZIPP-AIDS distributing sterile syringes, the prevention of AIDS will not be effective. The city council has organised a couple of bright-yellow vans that distribute sterile syringes a couple of hours a day and it also dispenses syringes through machines and pharmacies. But this is simply not the same as the ZIPP-AIDS project which even after Platzspitz was closed still had volunteers who would go out into the drug scene and hand out syringes, condoms, cotton swabs, and so on. Anyone who is desperate to shoot up and has not got a sterile syringe immediately available will simply use a used one.

What has also amazed me is that the repressive policies have led to the misuse of social welfare. The centre in which addicts are held until they can be sent back to their resident cantons or communes is really aimed at just getting the addicts off the streets with a kind of involuntary social welfare. I am very surprised that the Social Democratic Party has not been more critical about this.

The centre costs a lot of money and is an absolute waste of time – it achieves nothing. The people are picked up, are locked into the centre for 24 or 72 hours and then transported or sent back to their resident cantons. But the next day they are back in Zurich again. I tried to explain this to my colleagues in the city

council again yesterday. 'Give it a break. The repatriation to resident cantons is a waste of time, addicts go to wherever they can get
hold of the drugs.' I mean it's obviously a waste of time because
the communes where some of these addicts come from hardly have
any facilities for addicts; at most they might have an emergency
sleeping room for four people. So, of course, the addicts come
back to Zurich where the drugs are easier to get and where there
are more social welfare facilities. It simply does not work. Canton
Zurich wants to show that it is a progressive canton, but with this
measure it is not at all advanced. And this is certainly not a final
solution for the drug problem. Now the canton wants to set up a
closed clinic for addicts. I am afraid this is also a waste of time
and money. Taxpayers are simply having sand thrown in their eyes.

I believe in a liberal approach to drug addiction and I am
convinced that the only permanent solution to the problem is to
make it legal for people to buy and take drugs. I want to help
these people. I started helping them when I formulated a new
policy for drug addicts about ten years ago and managed to persuade the city government to introduce this programme. It is a
system of survival help with contact points, supervised sleeping
areas, emergency sleeping areas, supervised living centres and a
work programme. We have about six hundred people staying in
the supervised sleeping centres. In the work programme we have
ten job buses – they call it 'my fleet'. The buses pick up the people
in the morning and take them to one-day jobs and in the evening
they are brought back here to my offices and paid for their work.
Two months ago we started the pilot project, called Lifeline, in
Zurich for the medically-supervised distribution of heroin to 50
addicts.[5]

But all these measures are not sufficient to deal with the problem
satisfactorily. Legalisation of drug consumption, which is illegal in
Switzerland at present, is the best solution. I have believed in legalisation as the ultimate solution for some time. I am an economist
by training, not a social scientist, though I have always had socio-
political interests. Indeed that is how I came into politics in the
first place; originally I was a school teacher. But I saw very early
on that the drug problem would have to be solved on an economic
level. On the one hand we have prohibition, which favours illegal
dealing in drugs and enables enormous profits to be made. On the
other hand you have the poor developing countries where the drugs

are grown, for example in the Golden Triangle, where production is not a moral problem, it is part of their cultural heritage. Production in these countries is often run by the state or by agents of the state and they earn tremendous profits from the drugs trade. They then launder the profits through the Western financial system and use the money to buy weapons – often from the West.

The money and the weapons also end up in mafia and criminal circles like those we now see developing in the former Soviet Union. One has to ask oneself what is the aim of this drug dealing – of this international drug business – because this drug mafia is a very dangerous machine. And the only way we can deal with it is, just like in America during Prohibition, by removing the prohibition. Legalisation would not mean the total freedom to consume, but it would break and destroy the mafia-like nature of the drug market, the drug dealing itself. But it is not something we could do on our own here in Switzerland, it would have to be done all over the world. In reality it is exactly the same phenomenon as was seen in the alcohol Prohibition era in the United States in the 1930s. But so many people do not want to see this.

Of course, legalisation would not mean we would give up attempts to prevent drug addiction. About ten years ago I set up a centre for the prevention of drug addiction which has become a model for many countries in Europe. Even with legalisation prevention will be necessary – prevention is always necessary and we will always need therapy. But we must stop seeing drug consumption as something evil. It has become very clear that it is the conditions in which most people who consume drugs must live rather than the drugs themselves that result in addicts dying of overdoses, becoming tramps, disintegrating as individuals, being excluded from society and so on.

There are many doctors who will tell you that drugs alone do not kill. It is because people consume poor-quality drugs, because they no longer look after their own health, because they have to spend the whole day on the street in the scene, because they don't work any more, and because they turn criminal that addicts die so young. These conditions currently associated with drug consumption cause the desolation of drug addicts that we see today. It is not the drugs themselves that lead to these conditions. I certainly do not promote drug consumption – certainly not! When I go to the scene at Lettensteg and see the people, some of whom I have known for a long time, I always tell them to go into a rehabilitation programme. Often they say they have already tried that, to which I simply reply: 'Then try again! Where do you sleep? ... Here! Then go into one of our emergency sleeping shelters! Get a day job on one of our job buses!' That's how I talk to them.

My ideal is that people should be integrated into society and not excluded from it. I refuse to condemn anyone who takes drugs; I simply won't do it. The last time I was down at Lettensteg I met a young man whom I had last seen as a 16-year-old at one of the apprentice workshops that we organise. His is a typical story – a young man who may have committed a serious crime but who is not a bad person at heart. I have learnt over the years that often there is a bad family background, with terrible childhood experiences that you or I can hardly imagine. What kind of future does a 16-year-old who has been through these experiences and has been convicted of a crime see for himself? And then one day this young person, maybe he has just broken up with his girlfriend, tries out drugs.

Drug consumption has always existed and always will. We have to live with that. My goal is to build a society in which everyone is part of the society and is not excluded from it, a society in which everyone is supported by and at the same time supports their friends and neighbours. That may sound idealistic; it may sound unrealistic, even Utopian, but I believe in it.

Let me stress again, quite clearly, legalisation does not mean that one will be able to go to the corner kiosk and buy a small packet of heroin or ten cocaine cigarettes. Legalisation means consumption under legal control; it means the monopoly will lie with the state and not with the drug dealers. The state will not produce drugs itself, but it will arrange for drugs to be produced. And the state will determine where the drugs are to be distributed, how much, to whom, from what age, who will supervise the distribution – probably doctors or nurses in special clinics. For example, I would never give heroin to 13-, 14- and 15-year-olds.

But at the moment in Zurich legalisation is clearly not realistic. People are not yet ready to accept the ideal solution proposed. My alternative short-term solution is to move the drug scene to the outskirts of Zurich where it will no longer disturb city residents. The situation in the Industriequartier is clearly intolerable, with children going to school through an open drug scene and playing on the streets among drug addicts and blood-smeared syringes and so on. I originally made my proposal to move the scene outside Zurich to the city council about six months after Platzspitz was closed. But the council said it was out of the question because then there would have to be many more police on duty outside the city.

At the beginning of this year I reworked the proposal and said to my colleagues here in the social welfare department: 'I'll be retiring soon, but first I am going to leave a parting shot.' I then made this proposal public. I criticised the city council for its reactionary drug policy, also hoping to annoy the Social Democrats a little for their not having a sufficiently progressive drug policy. And I announced I would found a non-governmental group that would address the drug problem in Zurich on a private basis. A private group may be able to achieve a shifting of the drug scene out of the city more successfully than the government. The group will consist of prominent Zurich artists, other culturally active people, representatives of a lawyers' organisation and a number of other groups involved or interested in the drug problem. We will have to see how we finance ourselves, whether we set up a solidarity fund or whether we ask for donations. I already have my eye on two possible areas outside the city to which we could shift the scene.

Notes

1. The vote for women was not approved at the federal level in Switzerland until 1971 and it was not until the late 1980s that women were enfranchised in every Swiss canton.

2. Platzspitz is a small park on a narrow piece of woodland jutting into the Limmat river in central Zurich, a stone's throw from the city's central train station.

3. The Frankfurt Resolution was signed in November 1990 by the governments of Amsterdam, Frankfurt, Zurich and Hamburg. In it the cities agree to cooperate and exchange information on drug problems and policies.

4. The Zurich Intervention Pilot Project-AIDS (ZIPP-AIDS) was set up by a group of volunteers, led by a number of doctors at Zurich university. The group distributed sterile syringes, condoms, cotton swabs, and creams for damaged veins from a small hut in Platzspitz. The group hoped to relieve the misery of the addicts' existence and to limit the spread of AIDS among them. The volunteers also offered counselling to addicts and at the same time col-

lected statistical information on drug addiction at Platzspitz. After the closure of Platzspitz, government funding for ZIPP-AIDS stopped. For a while the group's volunteers would continue distributing sterile utensils among addicts by carrying backpacks full of syringes to Lettensteg.

5. In 1993 the Swiss federal government was the first national government to approve the distribution of heroin under medical supervision to addicts in a number of pilot projects in Swiss cities. Each project is limited to 50 addicts and is aimed at the most heavily addicted. Only addicts who have been on drugs for at least two years, who have made two unsuccessful attempts to break the addiction with methadone or other therapeutic programmes and who are at least 20 years old can participate in the projects.

THE VICAR

Ernst Sieber

Father Ernst Sieber has wild, unkempt white hair and a beard. He wears black jeans and a black leather jacket over a black waistcoat. His fingernails are dirty and there is dandruff on his shoulders. Often he breaks into a slow, infectious laugh; at other times he gazes into the distance and chews on his worn pipe before speaking. His appearance and manner belie his 66 years, except when he is walking when he moves very slowly. He is speaking at a table in an outdoor restaurant near the parliament in Berne and is often interrupted by strangers who recognise him from the newspapers or television and want to congratulate him on his work.

'My mother came from an old farmer's family which had worked the same farm for years in central Switzerland near Zug. I decided to study theology after working for a while as a farmer in a very lonely area where in the winter the river froze over and you heard no sound at all. I had always felt, from a very young age, that it was fun to work with the earth and that I wanted to be able to be close to the earth. And there on the land I felt that God was talking to me and that brought me to theology.

'In the 1960s I began working with the homeless after meeting some of the people who lived on the streets. I began spending more and more time on the problem of the homeless and later of the alcoholics and drug addicts, and had less and less time for my parish. Now I have retired and no longer have a formal church position but I am very busy at my centres for the homeless, alcoholics and drug addicts and in the parliament. My election to the parliament caused a bit of a flurry because article 75 of the Swiss constitution forbids clergy from sitting in the lower house of parliament.[1] The problem has always been solved in the past by clergy, who were elected into parliament, giving up the exercise of their clerical offices. In my case I had already retired when I was elected to parliament, but I continue to preach and still give sermons on radio and elsewhere. Nobody has complained yet. I have submitted a parliamentary initiative for this anachronistic article of the constitution to be changed so that every citizen of the country may be allowed to sit in parliament if elected. There will be a national referendum over this at some time in the future.

'I have four natural children and four adopted children. Initially the authorities would not allow me to adopt the four children I wanted to adopt because they said at the age of 31 I was too young. So I broke the law and simply smuggled the children across the Swiss border in my Citroën 2CV. This led to problems. The foreigners' police threatened they would put the four children in gaol. So I said: "Fine, I'll come with the whole family and you can lock us all up." Eventually I was given identity papers for the children which was absurd in a way because we did not even know when they had been born. But once I had the papers I was able to keep them without interference.'

We need to break out of the standard discussion of drugs or no drugs. I want to help addicts who want to leave the drug scene – their desire to leave is far stronger than most people realise – and I can only do that with my personal presence. I have a chain of centres in Switzerland for drug addicts, alcoholics and the homeless where I can have direct personal contact with these people. When I talk about helping them to leave the drug scene or about having contact with them in their daily lives, I do so purely out of religious conviction and because I see the addicts and homeless as my brothers and sisters.

The most important principle in my work is to be at the grass roots, which for me means close to the will of the individual. There have to be stations near the drug scene, so that there are fewer barriers preventing addicts from coming to us.

We don't use the Bible as a substitute opiate for addicts. Religious principles are not meant to enclose but to liberate. The approach is not just verbal – during my work as a vicar I never relied simply on the spoken word. I have often had doubts about naked theological language which can be so dry, barren and desiccated. If lessons come only from the pulpit then hearts will soon empty; religious principles must work in a liberating manner, just like all secular knowledge. It is a great mistake to try and imprison people with religious ideas. That happened in the twelfth and thirteenth centuries or even earlier when the churches locked God up in the monasteries. The religious principle underlying my stations is that those working there must be Christians, while the addicts or homeless who come for food and a place to sleep are not asked about their religion.

Apart from the basic stations which are near the drug scene, there is also – as a step further – one station where more rules are set. I am not of the opinion that I need to spread out my soul and allow people to walk all over it; I am also prepared to give orders. At this station the addicts live according to our rules and are supervised by us. The supervision is important, particularly at night, because we have to catch them if they get into breathing difficulties and make sure they do not choke on their own vomit if they throw up. For this centre, which started in January 1993, we had to go and pick the addicts up off the streets at first. But fairly soon a stable group of addicts who were keen to stay there developed and word also got round in the drug scene. Four months ago we introduced obligatory work duty at the centre. We simply announced it and most of the addicts then staying at the centre accepted it – a few said they did not agree with the new rules and left, and a couple have since been forced to leave because they have broken the rules or not completed the work duties. We usually have around twenty staying at the centre, but we hope to get permission from the commune to increase the number to 35.

The addicts are paid 20 francs for every day of work and they get a bonus of five francs if they complete the full day and another bonus if they complete the week with five full days of work. Every day they can choose whether they want to draw the money they have earned immediately or leave it with the office and build up their savings. The idea is to give them the feeling they are building something up in their lives and also to help them to learn a certain degree of self-discipline. We try to represent a very mild form of authority. Unfortunately most of the addicts here go straight to the drug scene after they have finished their work at the centre for the day and have got their money. But a couple do not and have come off drugs.

We do not allow people to shoot up in the centre, but we know that it is happening anyway. Of course, we tolerate this – we have to if we want to remain in touch with the drug scene. Also it gives us important information. If we find someone is shooting up on the premises and he or she is on a methadone programme, it may indicate that the methadone dose is not high enough. It may also show that the commitment of the workers in the centre needs to be improved. The commitment of these workers has to be very intensive, very intensive indeed.

This centre is the basis for a larger project I would like to start. The idea is to set up a village for drug addicts, or even a number of villages of around 60 people each, somewhere in Switzerland. But we would no longer be supervising it. The village would be self-administering and it would have to be largely self-sufficient, like a kibbutz. The theory is that in groups weaker members can lean on and have the support of stronger members, and the stronger members would be former drug addicts. I would live in the village at the start to help build it up. For people who had difficulties integrating into society or conforming with social norms when they were young, and who later also failed in society, a withdrawal from drugs and a return to society is probably impossible. Rather than leaving them as outcasts on the fringes of society we have to give them the opportunity of living according to their own values and in their own community rather than being strait-jacketed into conventional society. Maybe later they could live in the village and have jobs outside, I don't know. I am not sure that I am socialised into society, so I can hardly insist on a re-socialisation of addicts into society. I have presented a motion to the parliament for the federal government to provide land and money so that a village where addicts could live together can be set up in Switzerland.[2]

As far as legalisation is concerned it is interesting that former drug addicts all say we should never legalise heroin. I think the whole discussion about legalisation is premature because it tries to define the distant objectives when the more important immediate goals have yet to be achieved. Legalisation is no solution for the problem at all. It's just hell – I can say that because I was there on Platzspitz in 1988 and I saw the dead lying there and was with people as they died. Today I still see the dying because an AIDS centre is part of our network. It is more important first to help the addicts and the homeless, to ameliorate their immediate situation and immediate needs on an everyday basis rather than to discuss the advantages and disadvantages of legalisation.

The drug scene has undoubtedly worsened over the last twenty years. The addicts are physically weaker. It is harder to motivate them to participate in the voluntary work that we organise at a number of our centres. The drug scene has also become more violent and there is much more dealing going on now. The state has a role to play in helping to deal with the drug problem. My solution for the drug problem is on the one hand to work on the ground, close to the drug scene, and on the other hand to push for tougher measures by the state to control the supply of drugs and above all to punish those who are earning money from the drug scene – they are the ones who should be behind bars, not the addicts.

The cause of the drug problem in Switzerland is a complex matter. Historical factors are important and so are social and economic factors. I think we have to accept now that the problem and the solution must be seen in terms of society as a whole, the problem is not just an issue peripheral to so-called normal society. It is remarkable that the drug wave developed alongside the economic boom period. We cannot deny this. In Zurich, in Switzerland it is very clear that in the years of the youth revolt – in the 1970s, in the 1980s with the movement for the AJZ (*Autonomes Jugend Zentrum*) and in the 1990s with Platzspitz – the necessary responses to demands by young people were not made. Some of the young people participating in the troubles and protests of the 1970s and 1980s were from structurally poor areas where, after their education and training, they were not able to get the jobs they wanted because of unemployment. And in that kind of situation it is clear that there will be an increase in and a strengthening of drug addiction.

The growing wealth of the Swiss has definitely contributed to the drug problem in Switzerland. An individualism has developed over the years that is still with us. And people have become stubborn in dealing with the problem instead of being willing to open up to new ideas and to be freer in the search for solutions. Instead of talking about the drug addicts and those suffering under addiction one needs to talk with them and to include them in the planning and the discussion of the problem. When I talk to an addict in my AIDS centre it is not a question of me telling them what to do but of me responding to their questions. About 90 per cent of those questions come down to the question of the meaning of life.

I am not opposed to the pilot project in Zurich for a limited distribution of hard drugs under medical supervision because important and useful information will be gathered. But I have to say, as a spiritual adviser, that giving out hard drugs and gathering information is not the kind of approach to the problem that I favour because it does not allow for the meeting or encounter between two people that it is possible to have if one works on the street and near the drug scene.

The kind of work I do, the kind of work we do for the addicts, for the homeless and for the social outcasts can be very difficult and sometimes it is difficult to see the rewards or the goal. What I find most difficult is the sense of resignation that sometimes appears, when people working with me lose courage. I don't give up – I think that I was born with that quality – I am not able to give up, I can't. But sometimes the people working with me lose enthusiasm or courage.

Notes

1. Clergy were forbidden from serving the state or sitting in parliament in Switzerland's first federal constitution of 1848 which was passed following the brief Swiss civil war, the 1847 *Sonderbundskrieg*. The *Sonderbund* was an alliance of seven Catholic cantons, formed to oppose plans for stronger federal powers, which they feared would strengthen the hand of the mainly liberal Protestant cantons. The alliance was declared secessionist by the Federal Diet and in the brief war that ensued the *Sonderbund* was routed and its leaders forced to flee. The subsequent exclusion of clergy from serving in state offices was directed against the Catholics whose allegiance to the Swiss federal state was considered to be suspect after the *Sonderbundskrieg*. The 1848 constitution passed by the Federal parliament also outlawed the Jesuits who were alleged to have been behind the *Sonderbund* alliance.

2. The Swiss government in an initial reaction to the proposal said it had only found one piece of federal land in Switzerland which could be used for such a village and that it would not consider providing land or funds until the proposal had been worked out in detail.

THE DOCTOR

Werner Fuchs

Werner Fuchs, 47 years old, is a leading Swiss medical specialist on drug addiction. He was one of the founders of a radical AIDS prevention project, called Zurich Intervention Pilot Project-AIDS (ZIPP-AIDS), which was subsidised by the city government for three years between 1989 and 1992. The project was the high point of a liberal government policy towards drug addiction and addicts in the city which ended with the sudden closure of Platz-spitz, otherwise known as 'Needle Park' in early 1992. Fuchs has spent ten years in Zurich University's psychiatric clinic conducting research on the side-effects of methadone consumption.

He is currently working on a decentralised approach to dealing with drug addiction in a commune outside the city of Zurich. 'We are trying to see if it is possible to persuade drug addicts who live in this commune to stay here, rather than returning to the big open scene in Zurich, by offering them emergency sleeping quarters and a certain amount of assistance.'

Switzerland has one of the highest addiction rates in all of western Europe for all drugs, that is alcohol and hard drugs. For alcoholism alone Switzerland is ranked about third in western Europe. In fact Switzerland has traditionally been a country with high addiction levels. One of the reasons the country was an important centre for psychiatrists at the turn of the century was that many people were investigating the high rate of alcoholism here.[1]

The comparison with alcohol is a very useful one because it makes you realise that the whole problem with hard drugs has been greatly exaggerated when compared with the problem of alcoholism. The number of drug deaths we have every year in

Switzerland is minimal in comparison to the number of alcohol deaths and the social consequences and costs resulting from alcoholism and alcohol-induced accidents.[2] Alcohol is a much more brutal substance than opiates – with the exception, of course, of cocaine which is a very dangerous substance.

Nevertheless we do have a relatively high level of addiction to hard drugs in Switzerland. This cannot be denied. And no one knows why; we are all fumbling in the dark for reasons. Of course, there are many theories, some of which seem to make sense and seem plausible. For example there is the view that addiction is a reaction to Switzerland's extreme wealth or that it is a reaction to the society's inflexibility. But when investigatd in a rigorous scientific way there is not enough evidence or proof for any of these theories.

Although it is interesting to reflect on the reasons for addiction, if you want to deal with the problem you really have to accept drug consumption is a reality and that the question is not how to stop it but how to fit it into society. Drug addiction has become a fairly stable phenomenon in Switzerland. It is not true, as many people think, that the number of addicts is increasing and that consumption is growing. With the exception of cocaine, the consumption of all drugs has stabilised at the current relatively high level. As far as AIDS in Switzerland is concerned one also needs to be careful. The Swiss have a very good documentation and statistical system compared to many other European countries, so it is possible that the number of AIDS cases due to intravenous drug consumption may appear to be higher per capita here than in other countries because the statistics here are more complete than elsewhere.

But, if we want to integrate drug consumption into society, at the same time we need to get rid of the slum-like conditions and the social disintegration that drug addicts live in at the moment. It is probably impossible to completely eradicate these but at least we can try and minimise them.

When I talk about fitting drug consumption into society, however, I am not saying that drug addicts should be re-integrated into conventional society, get a job, start a family and have regular summer holidays. I do not think it is possible to lead drug addicts into a conventional existence while they are still on drugs, or only to a very limited extent. I am not even sure it is realistic to try and get addicts off drugs. My experience and my research into addiction tells me that it only makes sense to aim at damage limitation. The idea that the drug addiction problem could be solved if only the correct psychological and social assistance could be given to addicts leads very quickly to totalitarian attitudes and, therefore, I reject this approach completely.

The next question would be whether to legalise heroin and other drugs. If you can't solve the drug problem – just as you cannot solve many social problems but only limit or contain them – you then have to ask whether the legal distribution of these hard drugs would serve the goal of damage limitation. Yes or no? Such a step obviously entails risks as well as benefits. Therefore, I think it is absolutely right that Switzerland is running the pilot projects for the controlled distribution of drugs before it takes such a step, in order to see what advantages and disadvantages the legalisation of heroin, for example, would have. But one thing must be clear. These pilot projects will not solve the drug problem and will not lead to the disappearance of the drug scene from the streets. Both politicians and some drug therapists seem to believe this will be the case and they are wrong.

I am not a proponent of the legalisation of hard drugs. I am just interested in finding a way of bringing the consumption of drugs under control. In the case of other addictions, such as alcohol for example, consumption is under control in society; in the case of hard drugs it is not. No one is suggesting that hard drugs should be sold in supermarkets. It is clear that if there is to be any distribution of hard drugs it could only be via the medical system and infrastructure. But this approach will have its limits because it will require doctors to declare people to be patients before they can prescribe hard drugs for them, and many addicts will not accept this and say they are not patients but are normal.

However, even if you have prescription and distribution of drugs for addicts under medical supervision you will not get rid of the open drug scene – the open drug scene and legalisation of drugs are really two separate things. The open drug scene may get smaller if the state distributes drugs, but it will not disappear. All attempts made elsewhere to distribute drugs under supervision have not led to the disappearance of the drug scene. This is because the addicts in the scene are not only addicted to drugs but also to the sub-culture of the open drug scene, which has an attraction of its own.

The addicts have lost contact with their previous environment and have only this subculture to hang on to. It is not the case that addicts from all over Switzerland only go to the open scene in Zurich to get their daily fix, they can get that in many places. It is the scene itself in Zurich that attracts them. Medically supervised distribution of drugs will only help those addicts to leave the drug scene who are willing and ready to leave it.

But the legalisation and distribution of hard drugs under medical supervision still does not answer the question of how to deal with those addicts the programme does not reach. It will remain vitally important that addicts have access to therapeutic possibilities so that their lives and their health is stable, and they can at least live with drugs and lead a relatively normal life. It is here that there are far too many ideologues who argue only the one or the other is possible. One must see the whole thing in a much more differentiated manner and not simply as a question of drugs or no drugs.

In a way the plan at the time of the closure of Platzspitz was quite sensible. The idea was to suppress the open drug scene using the police and instead to encourage a backyard or private drug scene. The idea was based on the Dutch model which has been relatively successful in Amsterdam and which, accepting that there is no way to stop it entirely, allows drug consumption to go on while the 'normal' population is not disturbed by the eyesore of an open drug scene. Unfortunately in Zurich this private drug scene or private channel of supply and distribution does not seem to exist, so that the drug scene had to continue out in the open, and on the streets. The sudden closure of Platzspitz, without much notice and without any well-developed alternative infrastructure for the addicts, in fact led to the worst possible result. The addicts were simply chased a couple of hundred metres further away from Platzspitz to the abandoned railway siding at Lettensteg. And now if you go to Lettensteg you can see that the scene has become considerably more desolate than Platzspitz ever was. It is an absolute disaster!

The end of Platzspitz was also the end of ZIPP-AIDS unfortunately. We tried to continue the work for a while with our volunteers distributing syringes on foot in and around Lettensteg, but the city government had stopped our funding and we did not have the same contact with addicts that we had in Platzspitz when we were right at the centre of the scene from morning to late at night. Our experience with ZIPP-AIDS showed us that successfully to prevent the spread of AIDS and to understand the daily behaviour of addicts you have to have regular face-to-face contact, particularly with the young ones. This kind of contact is really only possible with something like ZIPP-AIDS which combined medical assistance with counselling. At ZIPP-AIDS, we would look at addicts' abscesses, bandage them and so on. We also offered hepatitis vaccinations which allowed us to get blood specimens from addicts.

The information we got from this face-to-face contact was invaluable. We discovered that the incidence of AIDS and HIV positive cases among drug addicts was not much higher in Switzerland than in other parts of Europe. Previously everyone had believed the AIDS problem to be much worse in Switzerland. We discovered that the number of HIV positive cases among young people under the age of 20 or people who had been consuming for less than one year was very low. But we also discovered that this was not because of a greater awareness of the risk of contracting AIDS by sharing needles since the level of hepatitis B infection among this group of people was very high. Hepatitis B is contracted in exactly the same way as HIV, only much more quickly, and this showed that the people in this group were probably sharing needles and infecting each other with hepatitis. So it was sheer good luck that almost none of these addicts who were sharing needles had contracted the HIV virus and infected others with it.

The lack of the face-to-face contact with addicts is a major loss. It means we will not be able to reach this group of young people or people who have only consumed for one year to educate them about the risks of AIDS and persuade them to change their drug consumption habits.

I am glad that I am not a politician, because I think politicians face a huge problem over Lettensteg – an enormous problem. The government is now operating a policy that is on very shaky legal ground, that is, the policy of picking up addicts who are not resident in Zurich and sending them back to their home communes. This is a clear infringement of civil rights.

I have no solution to offer. It is possible that if the government continues to make it unattractive for people to come to the drug scene addicts will gradually migrate away from Zurich. Also the repression makes the services offered by someone like Pfarrer Sieber more attractive to addicts. Much of the thinking now among therapists and policy makers is towards decentralisation, and getting addicts to stay in their home communes and so on. But one thing that is clear is it is not possible simply to get rid of the scene by force – the closure of Platzspitz showed that leads nowhere – the amount of force that would be needed means this is simply not a realistic option.

The message that needs to be spread to the general public is: drug addiction is a reality of our modern society and cannot be eradicated or removed. I think there is already a broad consensus among the population to accept such a view. But people always find it easier to accept something like that if they are not directly affected; if your children have to walk to school through an open drug scene then your tolerance may well be stretched beyond its limits.

Notes

1. A few of the prominent psychiatrists in Switzerland at the turn of the century were: Auguste Forel (1848–1931) who was a brilliant doctor and passionate advocate of abstinence and pacifism; Eugen Bleuler (1857–1939) who is responsible for the term and exact clinical description of schizophrenia; and Carl Gustav Jung (1875–1961) who developed analytical psychology.

2. According to government statistics the deaths of 419 people in 1992 and 353 in 1993 were due to the consumption of hard drugs. In 1992 some 890 people died either directly from alcohol consumption or due to alcohol-related causes. The number of deaths from illness or accidents which were influenced by alcohol consumption is estimated to be considerably higher.

Chapter 4

SWISS INDUSTRY: THE PROBLEM OF CONVENTIONS

The average Swiss needs to work a mere 20 minutes to earn enough for a hamburger and chips. An American would be at his desk for a full 26 minutes and a Mexican nearly four hours.[1] The Swiss are wealthier than most, regardless of whether you measure average salaries, per capita gross domestic product or the cost of their fast food.

Once among Europe's poorest countries with a population that at the beginning of the twentieth century was underfed and forced to emigrate, Switzerland has now become one of the world's wealthiest nations. Most of the growth came after World War Two. The country's export industries were able to meet demand that the exhausted and devastated economies of Europe were unable to supply. Fixed exchange rates and an undervalued currency made Swiss goods competitive. Plentiful capital resources, lent at the lowest rates in Europe, added to Swiss companies' competitive edge. Discreet and secure Swiss banks, which became a haven for the savings of dictators, the persecuted and for tax flight, were at times so cash-rich they were able to charge depositors negative interest rates. Cheap foreign labour, mainly from Mediterranean countries, helped to restrain wage rises, and Switzerland's deeply-rooted political consensus spared it the radical politicisation of industrial relations that hit many other western European countries in the 1970s.

But times have changed and many Swiss are worried these advantages have evaporated. An economy long built on low inflation, full employment and the comforting stability of cartelised markets is having to grapple with the highest unemployment since World War Two, cut-throat competition and the nagging fear that things may be taking a turn for the worse. Leading bankers and industrialists warn that Switzerland faces a threat from increasingly competitive European and Asian economies, and that it must reshape economic and political structures if it wants to preserve prosperity. 'We have far too much of the feeling that we have a God-given right to the highest living standard in the world,' the chairman of one of the country's largest financial services groups said, explaining the malaise.[2]

The Swiss watch industry is one of the best and earliest examples of the clash between outdated industrial structures and attitudes on the one hand and modern competitive markets on the other. For centuries Switzerland led the world in the clocks and watches business. The Huguenots fleeing Catholic persecution in France in the seventeenth century first brought the clock maker's skills to Switzerland and soon a number of manufacturers had settled in western Switzerland. By the 1970s the Swiss watch industry seemed impregnable. It controlled more than half of the world market, employed around 10 per cent of the country's industrial labour force and accounted for over 10 per cent of Switzerland's total exports. Its largest single manufacturer, Asuag (*Allgemeine Schweizerische Uhrenindustrie AG*), which was a conglomerate of various small watch- and component-makers, was the country's ninth largest industrial company.

Yet the seeds of the downfall had already been planted. Lulled into complacency by its dominance the Swiss watch industry developed quartz technology but then discarded it, considering it a fad without commercial value. The Japanese did not. Soon millions of cheap quartz watches made in Japan and, a little later, Hong Kong were flooding the world market. Swiss watch exports plummeted from a high of 91 million units in 1974 to 43 million by 1983. In the same period half the industry's jobs were cut and a quarter of the country's watch-making companies collapsed.

By the early 1980s Asuag and SSIH (*Société Suisse pour l'Industrie Horlogère*), the country's largest and second-largest manufacturers respectively, were in severe difficulties and banks had to step in with emergency loans. Opinions were divided over whether the Swiss industry should concentrate on market niches and only produce expensive, high-quality watches or whether the Japanese dominance in the mass market should be challenged. One of the companies in the Asuag group decided to try and compete with the Japanese. ETA, managed by a new industry *wunderkind* called Ernst Thomke, used technology – developed by the Swiss to produce the world's thinnest watch in 1981 – to design and manufacture a cheap watch sealed in a synthetic case: the Swatch. The revolutionary Swatch process used robots to insert metal parts directly into a plastic case before sealing it rather than following the usual three-stage procedure in which case and mechanism were made separately and then joined together. The new watch had far fewer moving parts compared to other battery-powered watches.

Swatch was on the market by 1982, but early sales were slow. And fundamental problems in the Swiss watch industry remained unsolved. Nicolas Hayek, a dynamic, Lebanese-born entrepreneur who had been called in to advise the banks on how to restructure the industry, proposed a merger of Asuag and SSIH. By 1985 the merged company had been renamed *Société Suisse Microelectronique et d'Horlogerie* (SMH) and Hayek, who was convinced the Japanese could be beaten, was running it. The turnaround has become a legend. In 1983 the Asuag–SSIH merger had sales of around 1.5 billion francs and made a loss of about 170 million. Ten years later the company had sales of about 2.8 billion and made a profit of 441 million francs.

Hayek has since been widely seen as the saviour of the watch industry. Although some mutter that it was Thomke not Hayek who developed the Swatch technology, the marketing genius of Hayek, who cultivates an image of provocative unconventionality to match the Swatch, undoubtedly helped the industry back on to its feet. But regardless of whether he saved the industry single-handedly or not, many see Hayek as an example of the creativity and unconventionality that is lacking in Swiss industry in general. As Fritz Leutwiler, a former president of the Swiss National Bank, once said: 'We need more Hayeks.'[3]

While Hayek was saving the watch industry another pillar of the Swiss economy was in trouble. Oerlikon-Buehrle was a family business founded in the early twentieth century, which had rapidly expanded to become the main weapons supplier to the Swiss army as well as to the Chinese and Spanish Civil Wars and to Nazi Germany during the Second World War. By the mid-1980s, however, due to a combination of poor management and sharp reductions in weapons sales as Cold War tensions eased, the company had nosedived into a spiral of falling sales and profits.

By 1990 the banks had taken control and forced the family out of the operational management. Hans Widmer, a former director of the Swiss chemical giant Sandoz who had gained a reputation as a turnaround specialist, was appointed chief executive in 1991. By 1992 he had radically cut costs and brought the company back to profit after six straight years of losses.

Both Hayek and Widmer are mavericks, critical of many Swiss industrial practices and intolerant of conventions. Here, in separate interviews, Hayek explains his marketing philosophy and the problem of management structures, while Widmer assesses the strengths and weaknesses of Swiss industry.

Notes

1. Enz (1991), p. 10.

2. Rainer Gut, chairman of CS Holding, a major diversified financial services group, in an interview with Swiss newspaper, *Finanz und Wirtschaft*, 26 June 1991.

3. Quoted in Altwegg (1993).

MR SWATCH

Nicolas Hayek

Nicolas Hayek, 65, exudes a huge and overwhelming charisma. He is short, has bushy black eyebrows that meet over his nose and has grey, thinning hair. While talking he rolls up one sleeve of his suit, opens the shirt cuff and folds it back to show three watches he is wearing on his forearm. He speaks at a large round glass table in his office, switching frequently and easily between German and English. Frequently he uses a notepad to illustrate what he is saying, tearing off each sheet once it is full. A number of awards for SMH products are displayed on the window sills. The telephone – a Swatch telephone made by SMH – rings and he answers in a flat, quiet monotone that contrasts completely with his otherwise exuberant manner. The call is from the United States and is a request for an interview.

Hayek was born in Beirut to an American professor father and a Lebanese mother. He studied physics and mathematics in France and planned to specialise in nuclear physics in the United States. However, his father-in-law, who ran a foundry in Switzerland, suddenly became seriously ill and Hayek had to step into the breach. Later the father-in-law recovered and soon the two were disagreeing with one another over how to run the business. Hayek left, founded a consulting firm called Hayek Engineering and travelled to Germany to look for the clients that he could not find in Switzerland. Soon he was advising major German conglomerates – Mannesmann, Thyssen, Audi and Daimler Benz. In 1985 he became chairman of SMH.

It is very important for me that I fulfil whatever I promise. A person with my kind of optimism tends immediately to give people confidence. If people are unhappy about something and they talk to me, usually they feel much better. I don't want to disappoint the confidence people place in me. You see my problem is the small investor, the pensioner who invests his or her life's savings in shares in my company because they have seen how the share price has been going up and up and up over the last five years. If the share falls 2.50 francs they immediately write me a letter and complain about how much money they have lost, and that I should have warned them and that I should do something about it. I've never even met these people and they are writing me these letters. I get letters from people in Germany, France and Italy – practically from all over the world – and many just tell me the stories of their lives.

As an entrepreneur I don't like disappointing people. So often people in our society doubt that we can achieve what we set out to do, simply because it seems so difficult to achieve. But calculated risk taking and the will to overcome difficulties are important to the development of new things and wealth. It was like that with the Swatch watch and it is like that with the Swatch car project[1] now. I think when we started SMH and the Swatch the public, including the banks, did not really believe that it would be possible for Switzerland to produce and sell watches as mass market consumer goods and to compete with low-cost areas like Japan and Hong Kong. That is why, when in 1985 I and a group of investors exercised an option, we had to take a 51 per cent stake in SMH.

The beginnings of SMH came in 1983. The banks had asked me at Hayek Engineering to advise them on the future of the two largest watch companies. The question was whether to close the companies down or how, if it was possible, to save the Swiss watch industry. Based on what I recommended it was decided to aim at becoming the world leader in the industry and to do so by merging the country's two big watch manufacturing groups, which were both in trouble, into one company. By 1985 that had become Asuag-SSIH and now it is SMH. The two manufacturers, SSIH and Asuag, were both making losses. They were both incredibly inefficient, and had costs that were far too high, and had made serious strategic and management mistakes.

To understand what was going on in the international watch industry at that time you need to imagine a wedding cake with three tiers. When the banks came to me for advice the Swiss had completely lost their share of the bottom tier, the low-price mass market segment representing 90 per cent of the total number of watches produced. They had a very small share of the middle tier, covering about 8.5 per cent of the units sold, and had almost all of the top tier, representing the market for a small amount – about 1.5 per cent of the total market – of very high-quality watches.

SMH is vertically integrated. We produce all the components that we need for our watches. We don't just produce simple nuts and bolts, but strategic components that no one else makes. The *Harvard Business Review* says we are like a juggernaut, a vertically integrated fortress. This gives us strategic independence and makes sure we are not at the mercy of any producer of a particular component.

SMH is now the indisputable world leader in watches. Let me give you some figures to show you. SMH produces approximately 100 million watches and watch movements a year. The previous record of the Swiss watch industry was 91 million in 1974. We have broken that record. But how do we compare with the Japanese? About 55 to 60 per cent of our total production is finished watches, the rest being just movements. Of the movements, over three-quarters are expensive movements and cost between 20 and 500 Swiss francs apiece. The rest are very cheap and are sold to the Hong Kong watch manufacturers and these cost between 2.70 and 3.50 francs each – they are just a cheap commodity. One of the larger Japanese producers makes 260 million watches and movements. About 10 to 12 per cent of their production is finished watches and they sell all the rest to Hong Kong. So that means if we are just talking about finished watches they make far fewer than we do. We make about 60 million finished watches and they make fewer. Another Japanese producer, which says it is the biggest watch producer in the world, makes 300 million watches and movements a year, with about 5 to 7 per cent being finished watches and the rest going to Hong Kong. So that leaves SMH as the world's largest producer of finished watches by money value.

Although Swiss watch production is still concentrated in the upper tiers of the 'wedding cake' we have reversed the trend of the 1970s and 1980s with the Swatch and now have a significant share of the bottom tier – the mass market. We achieved this because, unlike the Japanese watches, Swatch not only has an image but also gives a very clear emotional message to consumers.

We have such a warm-hearted message that it appeals to

everyone. There are very many people who develop an image for their companies and products – a corporate image. Benneton is a good example. But very few have an image and a message behind the image. To show you the difference between an image and a message, take the following example; it may seem stupid, but I can't think of a better one. Imagine a room and in the room you have a healthy young man, a healthy young woman who is his girlfriend or wife and a healthy young homosexual. The man opens a magazine and sees a photo of a beautiful, well-proportioned woman. What is the normal reaction that he will have 99 per cent of the time? 'Attractive. I would like to meet her,' is what he thinks or says. The reaction of his girlfriend or his wife when she sees the same photo is: 'You are just as stupid as most men. You haven't noticed that she is cross-eyed, has dyed her hair blonde and has tons of silicon on both sides of her chest.' And she will hate this image. And the homosexual will think: 'My goodness, why do they show women as if they are milk cows?' So what do we have? We have a passive, reproducible image and two out of three people are against it and reject it, while one out of three likes it.

I didn't want to have two out of every three against me so I decided our low-cost Swiss watches needed a clear active message and not just a passive image if they were to beat the Japanese. What is a message? A message is when that woman in the picture comes into the room and delivers a true message, and the message must be perceived as being true. It is incredibly important for me that my message to the public is true and that I keep my promise. It is vital that this real message has a meaning and is not empty. It is no good for this woman to come into the room and say: 'I am the most beautiful'. That is a waste of time. It must be a message with substance and also it must be short – if she gives a long speech everyone in the room will fall asleep. The message must be warm-hearted; I can't emphasise this point enough here, for the Swiss. People have forgotten that tourists and other people are our clients and that this warm-heartedness should not be affected or false but genuine.

So how do the three people in the room react now? The young man will say: 'Ah ha, an attractive, warm-hearted and intelligent woman who has something sensible to say. I must get to know her.' He doesn't say he would like to get to know her but that he 'must'. The wife or girlfriend will say: 'This is an honest, intelligent and interesting woman, who is not simply after my man. I can trust her and should try and get to know her.' The homosexual will think: 'She looks interesting and she could become a friend, I should get to know her.' So the chances are quite good that this woman will be accepted by two, or two and a half, or possibly three out of three people, especially if the message is true, intelligent and warm-hearted enough.

Each of the 11 different brands of watches produced at SMH, whether expensive or cheap, must have a message: a very distinctive, different message. Let me give you an example. What is the message behind Swatch? First, Swatch is high quality. When we first launched Swatch, as part of the promotion I smashed them against a wall in front of the media to show how strong they were. We also had them suspended in a goldfish aquarium to show how waterproof they were. Second, Swatch is low in cost. We have never raised the price of the Swatch since it began production. The basic Swatch has always been 50 Swiss francs. The price sensitivity in this market segment is very great. We sell the Swatch Chrono for 100 francs even though we can hardly meet the demand at this price. But we keep this price to keep our message true. Third, Swatch conveys provocation or challenge, but also a kind of enjoyment of life. My personal state of mind has always been to oppose and challenge conventions. Fourth, Swatch production is undertaken in a Western industrial country. But we never make that part of our public message; we just say that it is Swiss-made. We must get away from the idea that a company producing for a mass market can only produce in low-wage countries in Asia or South America. If we manage to keep labour costs below 10 per cent of total costs, we can produce anywhere – in Switzerland, in the most expensive countries in the world. And that is how we produce the Swatch. The people who designed the Swatch and the technology to produce it were the best in the world and they came from Switzerland. The final part of the message is that the product must be sellable everywhere, throughout the whole world.

And we use that message when marketing our products anywhere in the world, for example, in Germany and Japan where we set up huge working models of a Swatch and hung them from big grey skyscrapers in Frankfurt and in Tokyo. The models gave the essence of the message – Swiss quality, the low price, the name, and at the same time provocative because no one else had thought of setting up a huge, low-cost watch on a very expensive bank skyscraper.

So that is Swatch. And there are very few people who understand the concept – the message – that is Swatch. So many people write to me saying things like: 'I have a hotel; I want to call it Swatch; how much will it cost?' There were some students who came to me after they had worked for a US consultant for three years and said they had a proposal to set up a chain of hotels and name them Swatch. And I said: 'Look, your hotels will have to be the best quality there is but will have to charge very low prices and, just to start with, how do you intend to achieve that with costs the way they are in Switzerland and Germany? And then they would have to be provocative. What are you going to do in your hotels that is so provocative? And they would have to be sellable everywhere, which means you would have to build up your chain of hotels in a matter of six months around the whole world.'

You can use the Swatch recipe for some goods but not for all. It works for emotional consumer goods but don't try to sell a nuclear power station or a Kalashnikov rifle as a warm-hearted, provocative, fun, high-quality, low-cost product.

The Swatch message is, of course, at the centre of my Swatch car project. And it was partly the problem of the message that led to the parting of ways with Volkswagen.[2] Some people ask me why I started talking publicly about my car project some time ago before I had already settled on a partner. They think I am just using the car project as a way of promoting and marketing the Swatch watch. But that is not true. I had to start publicising the project because I needed a 'pull message' for three different groups of people. The first group is people who have ideas. From Sweden to south Italy, from all over the world wherever the Swatch is sold, we have millions of people who have technical ideas about cars and I needed to attract their attention. The second group is the companies that make components. We needed to tell them that if they helped to develop the components for the project at their own expense then they would have the first chance to be the suppliers on competitive terms when the project was up and running. And the third group is the car producers whom we need for their access to markets. If I developed the car on my own and tried to sell it in Britain, for example, the authorities would take every screw apart before they would allow us to sell it there. In France, Germany and in America it is the same story, even if you have a good product. We also need the distribution systems of the big car manufacturers. Unfortunately I won't be able to sell the car in jewellery shops.

But we are in rather a unique situation now, because we never believed the idea would take such an enormous hold on the minds of the public when I first spoke about it. I had expected to announce that we were planning to develop and produce a car and then to be left alone for at least seven years, which is normally the time you need to develop and produce a new car. But the public expectation and the press are not leaving me alone, constantly saying: 'Hayek is lying, there is no car.' So then I tell the media: 'We have a prototype and it has been driven by Mr Bangemann of the European Commission and by M. Chirac of France.' Then the press says that I have a prototype but that I have no partner. Recently someone asked me why SMH does not build the car on its own. The government of a major country is prepared to help us build a factory for the car and the Swiss authorities would help us build a factory for components. But we are not after a quick solution that will give us cheap, immediate, public recognition; we want a car that will be a success. And if it has to happen after my death, that is also okay as long as it is a real success for the whole of humanity.

We are negotiating with two partners at the moment. One of the partners is our preferred partner, but the second is just as good. The crucial problem is the issue of the message. Car producers today use their name to produce a large range of products with the same message. At SMH we have 11 different brands for 11 different products. Of course it would be much easier if we were to take the name Omega and produce an expensive Omega, a baby Omega and use Omega for all types of SMH watches. But then I would not have the separate message or concept for each brand that is so important if you want to sell the products successfully.

Among the few car producers who have really understood this are General Motors and Fiat. Fiat has not tried to make Fiat-Alfa Romeo cars, or Fiat-Ferrari cars, or Fiat-Lancia cars, in fact, few people know that Alfa Romeo, Ferrari and Lancia all belong to the Fiat group. Each of the brands has a very distinct individual identity and message. How would you react if Rolls-Royce said they were producing a mini-Rolls-Royce for £12,000? That's how trademarks are killed; that's how messages are killed. People don't understand the message any more. You must never change the message of a product. We developed and built up the messages of each of our watches and we don't want to kill any of them. That is how the message behind Omega was gravely wounded in the 1970s, though is has happily revived in the last seven years. SSIH tried to expand by selling Omegas in the low- and medium-price range and they greatly damaged the message that Omega had had until then of a prestige, quality, luxury watch. Four or five years ago we had an offer – and this is no joke – of one billion dollars for the name Swatch. An offer under which we could have kept the name for our watches and they would have used them for a range of consumer products. Of course I refused. It would have been a disaster for Swatch.

Why do you think I want to build cars rather than produce toothpaste or vacuum cleaners? There are two reasons really. First the Swatch car is the kind of development, the kind of step, that mankind must take. We have to do it whether we want to or not. It is quite clear if we continue using our current cars and the Hindus, the Chinese and the Russians demand the same degree of mobility that we in the West have now, we will soon run out of oxygen on this planet. And by the time that happens it will be the earth of our children and our grandchildren. So if we want to save them, we have to do something now. Secondly today's consumer wants an ecological car that has all the characteristics of a normal car, that is high quality but low cost, but does not look like a soap box on the street like the cars at present which are more obstructions than anything else. We have researched it and analysed it and we are quite sure that it is feasible. Nobody else seems to dare to make it. Society, because of the organisational structures that it has created, has become lazy and uninspired and lacks creativity. But we are still creative and we are neither lazy nor lacking in inspiration. So we are going to do it.[3]

One of the most inhuman things that we have in the industrial world is organisational structures. We all have the ability to be innovative, to think creatively, but it is destroyed by organisational structures. As children we have innovation and over time it is destroyed, but thank God not in all of us. I always say that every chief executive and every one of us should have the creativity, fantasy and curiosity of a six-year-old. What do I mean by inhuman structures? I'm talking about government and huge companies, particularly some car companies; all of them are huge, even the smallest ones. Let me give you an example. If you open a banana kiosk at the central train station in Zurich then you need common sense and 1,000 francs, no more. You buy the bananas, you sell the bananas and pocket the profit. But if your wife says she wants to open a banana kiosk at the airport as well, you need a small system. You need to communicate with each other. If you have already sold all your bananas at the train station by 10 a.m. and she has not sold a single one at the airport then you need someone who will bring the bananas from the airport to the train station or you will need some other solution. Then you and your wife decide you will expand and open 20,000 kiosks in all of Switzerland with 20,000 different products – bananas, apples, chocolate, newspapers, chewing gum, cigarettes and so on – then you have a situation in which common sense and gut feeling is not enough to control and develop such a complex system. So what do we do? We are forced to introduce this darned inhuman thing, this system, which is against the natural instinct of human nature. And most of the world's large companies have organised their systems according to a consultant or a university or an army model, with so many hierarchies that the individual person cannot think, act or react any more in normal sensible ways like a normal, sensitive, intelligent human being.

At SMH we avoid this as much as possible. We determine what tasks are the relevant and crucial ones required to control this system and then we concentrate on those – and only those tasks and no others. The SMH group is controlled by 45 people, no more. And don't forget we are a company which is present in every region of the world. We take the approach of asking, like children do, why are we doing something rather than simply doing it because everyone else is doing it. But now you see one of the reasons why several large car companies find it difficult to produce a car that is truly new, that is different from the cars they have produced for the last fifty years. They need a push because most have forgotten how to be quickly and simply creative; they are locked into their bureaucracies and are so busy organising that they can't really innovate any more.

My job in the SMH organisation is many-faceted. First, my job is to encourage people and motivate them. Second, it is to bridge the chasms between the precise German Swiss who produce watches down to the smallest micromillimetre and the designers who are absolute artists, between the serious-minded financiers we have and the risk-friendly entrepreneurs and developers of ideas. I have to keep all these different people under one umbrella and keep the company open and not restrictive to the work of each individual. It is not easy to win the respect of and be a model for all the people working in such an exciting company.

Above all we have to avoid management mistakes that would make our products unfeeling and grey, or make the consumer stop buying our products, or force us to raise the prices, or cause us to become arrogant, or make us underestimate the competition.

I have four important qualities for this company. I am very experienced in industrial processes, that is production, planning, steering, productivity, personnel, and how to get a product through the company more quickly. Second, I am an experienced marketing and sales person. I can sell well. I can demonstrate well. Third, I'm ferociously honest in the sense that for example when I want a watch from SMH I pay for it and don't say: 'I am a head guy; I don't need to pay.' Fourth, I have the necessary warm-heartedness and emotion to bind strong men and women together. I am not the kind of person who says: 'Go to the front, there's shooting there,' while I stay behind the lines. I go along. I say: 'Right kids, now we are going to shoot or push or charm our way through.'

This is a culture you pump into a company and I will go on doing it as long as my health and vitality allow. And my health does allow it – I have always been like a tiger. Despite my good health the board of directors and I have formulated contingency plans for what would happen if I were to have an accident. But as long as there is no accident I am going to be around. Hopefully I will die on my feet. Among other things I feel I am the father of SMH and I am emotionally tied to the company.

Notes

1. SMH and Volkswagen announced in 1991 that they planned to design and produce a small, low-cost, environmentally-friendly city car with enough room for two people and a case of beer. The car would either be electric-powered, or run on a hybrid engine that would switch to petrol or diesel propulsion for higher speeds.

2. Volkswagen and SMH announced in January 1993 that they were ending their cooperation for the development of the Swatch car.

3. On 4 March 1994, SMH and Mercedes Benz announced their cooperation in a joint venture to produce a small city car. Mercedes is providing a prototype it had been developing for some time and SMH will develop components and motor systems for the cars' electronics as well as provide the name Swatch and a marketing concept.

THE ENTREPRENEUR

Hans Widmer

Hans Widmer, 54 years old, is of medium height, balding and has drawn, almost haggard features. He sits in an immaculately tidy office at a round glass table. In front of him is a pen and pad which he frequently uses to illustrate his words with rough diagrams. He crosses and uncrosses his legs frequently and speaks clearly and precisely, occasionally interrupting to throw a question back at the questioner. The door of his office is open and he acknowledges colleagues who enter and, seeing he is busy, leave again. Occasionally he clasps his hands behind his head. A former director of the management consultancy McKinsey Company in Zurich, he has been chief executive officer of Oerlikon-Buehrle since April 1991. Widmer says yoga is very important to him. 'Once a week I have a teacher for one hour and every other day I do 20 minutes of yoga alone. Yoga is good for me as relaxation and an anti-stress technique.'

The strengths and weaknesses of Swiss industry? That is very straightforward. We Swiss succeed in the world economy if we concentrate on developing ideas; the world is full of manual labour, but what is missing are ideas and intellect. If you correlate the content of ideas and the success of Swiss companies then you get a very clear picture. Chemical firms are the firms with the greatest content of ideas in industry; and the chemical industry is the most successful in Switzerland, being the country's second largest export sector. Idea-intensive work involving ideas of another kind is the creation of a brand name, for example like Bally (fashion and shoe division of Oerlikon). I can't spread a brand name around the world from Korea. I see in the case of the Japanese car industry that their best products do not sell well in the world because the intellectual aspect of the identification with the product is missing. Nobody wants to identify themselves with a Japanese product. With Bally there is a fantastic chance through work here in Switzerland to generate value for the identity of Bally and the presentation of Bally in the world.

Then there are also possibilities in mechanical engineering or, for example, in our own aircraft construction to do highly technical work. But we will only survive as long as we concentrate on developing intelligence and training. As soon as we start fastening nuts and bolts with our expensive hands, for example in aircraft construction, the business is finished. We originally wanted to produce the PC-XII in Switzerland for $1.75 million[1] but we found that the aircraft would only be competitive if it was a third cheaper. So we produced the undercarriage in Israel, the cabin in Portugal, and so on, and now the plane costs $1.25 million. Because we took this manual work elsewhere, where other hands can do it better and cheaper, we were able to concentrate on the intellectual work, which we like to do and which we are good at. This is the direction Switzerland must take.

A very audacious possibility for Switzerland lies in the example of Nestlé – the Swiss as the entrepreneurs of the world, like the Armenians and Jews. If I consider the demand for this kind of leadership through ideas, we would have enough jobs for twice the population of Switzerland. Take the Ukraine with a population of 40 to 45 million: the country has vast and wide-ranging natural resources and plenty of universities, and their people, as consumers, have reached the level of consciousness and development at which they demand the same things that we demand in the West – compact discs, refrigerators, televisions, cars and so on. So what is missing in the Ukraine? The entrepreneur who wants to get the whole thing moving! At the moment Nestlé goes to many low-wage countries and starts up food factories with local workers. Nestlé could also go into the Ukraine and buy acres of farmland, it would have the financial power to do that, and take advantage of the excellent natural resources and the well-educated and cheap labour there. It is in this sort of area that I see the possibilities for Switzerland. If you look at the amount of direct Swiss investment abroad you will be amazed at how much power Swiss entrepreneurs have abroad or even how much influence a handful of people in Vevey[2] have.

But what is completely out of the question is for us to do banal manual work for the high salaries that we pay ourselves. If we want to do such work, we will have to lower the high salaries we pay ourselves.

It is, for example, ludicrous to operate spinning mills in Switzerland. But the companies that do, do so because they already have the weaving machines, they have already depreciated them, they have cheap foreign labour working the machines and they are able somehow to make ends meet. The case is similar for middle-range industrial production, for example producing 100 aircraft in Stans and fixing the rivets ourselves. That's a waste of time. Machine-tool engineering also no longer works in the old way. These operations are only feasible if the marketing or the financing is done here and the actual manual labour, which can be done by moderately well-trained labour anywhere in the world, is done abroad – for example in China. If you look at Rieter, Saurer[3] and so on, they are now building production capacity in suitable areas overseas. They keep some of the idea capital here in Switzerland. Sewing machines in Steckborn?[4] Absolutely out of the question. Most sewing machine producers are in Taiwan and have been for many years, though the cleverest ones have in fact left Taiwan and are now in Communist China. The globalisation of industrial production in today's world means that the work goes to the cheapest producer.

I disagree with the argument that Swiss entrepreneurs lack creativity. Whenever I am confronted with that argument I always ask what the yardstick is. I don't think we are necessarily less creative than entrepreneurs in any other European country. I don't want to be arrogant, but equally I don't want to be defeatist. The Swiss entrepreneurial spirit not only occupies and provides jobs for hundreds of thousands of people abroad through the billions of francs of direct investment abroad by Swiss companies, it also provides jobs for over a million foreigners in Switzerland. It is too easy to say that there are not enough entrepreneurs in Switzerland or that the entrepreneurs are not creative enough. I could go home every evening and say to myself: 'God you were lazy today. You should have had three times as many ideas as you had or you should have had the ideas you had in eight hours in one hour.' It's not always that easy to be creative.

The arguments that the cartels and cartel-like thinking in Switzerland constrain creativity and make for conformity are also clichéd. Are the unions in Germany or the support for medium-sized enterprises in Germany with federal and state subsidies any better? And in the European Union if someone develops a new product, a revolutionary electronic programme for example, they first have to toddle off to Brussels and spend time there ensuring they can get subsidies for its development rather than spending the time developing the product further. Almost wherever you look you see too many restrictive structures.

This is true of Switzerland as well. You can divide the Swiss economy into three parts: industry, the trades and professions, and the state. Only industry has contact with the outside world and it is kept fit every day because that is the only way that it can survive. The trades and professions do not face this challenge, and we have by far the most expensive trades and professions in the world as a result. The state also does not face competitive challenge and, similarly, has costs that are far too high.

What is the result? If industry is 100 per cent efficient, the professions 70 per cent and the state 30 per cent efficient, industry has to carry the inefficiency of the professions and the state in its competition with the outside world. This is where Switzerland must improve. The Swiss government could very easily get its finances back into order if there was the will to do it. The eight billion francs deficit that they are complaining about could be solved in one afternoon.[5] With the trades and professions I am not so sure how you would go about it. They have become very comfortable because they have a geographical monopoly, whether we're talking about doctors, lawyers or coffin makers. With every crisis the professions become more recession-resistant because they react in a cartel-like manner rather than trying to reduce costs. Hiding behind cartels is not a solution in the long term, of course. Ascom is a perfect example of what happens if you rely on cartels.[6] I see our state and our trades and professions as institutions that are very bad for Switzerland. These areas of the economy must be liberalised.

But again, what is the yardstick? Although we are certainly much worse than we could be in these areas I don't think we are much worse off than the countries around us. And I still say that it is too easy to claim that Switzerland lacks creativity and innovation because it became comfortable after the Second World War when huge capital inflows made investment capital cheap. It's possible that this exists as well, but I do not think it is the most serious problem we have.

I can think of at least one problem that is more serious and that is our atrophied boards of directors. There is a widespread view here in Switzerland that when an executive retires then he can spend a bit of time amusing himself on a couple of boards of directors. Recently I was with a group of 20 managers who had been brought together to exchange their experiences in dealing with Switzerland's most difficult companies. We were supposed to be the managers with the most difficult turnarounds. I asked them what their main problem had been in getting their companies back into profit, what their core problem had been. About 60 per cent of them said the root difficulty had been the owner, or the chairman of the board, or the board itself. It is always the same – either a board has no vision, is incompetent, or it is dominated by a single figure who built up the company and who cannot accept that he or she must step down to make way for new ideas and new people.

I see no problem with having a director on the board who is, say, a lively 40-year-old, financially independent and so not on the board for the money, and completely committed to the company – we have such a board member at Oerlikon-Buehrle. But in Switzerland there's a lack of board directors of true quality and a lack of understanding about what a board of directors should be doing. It is not so much a problem that some directors have too many directorships but that the incompetence of their work is so great.

The incompetence is often not due to the person him- or herself, but to the manner in which many boards carry out their responsibilities as directors. At one company that I had contact with, I won't mention the name, the board met four times a year. The directors arrived at eight o'clock in the morning, looked at the agenda and at nine o'clock the meeting started. Lunch was at one o'clock and until then all the director had to do was make sure he did not fall asleep, or ask any cheeky or awkward questions. An example of the kind of questions that were allowed is: 'Does this beta-blocker also open the vessels in the periphery?' The answer would be 'yes'. The chairman would ask: 'Is the questioner satisfied?' And he would answer: 'I am not satisfied, I am euphoric!

Ha, ha, ha!' In this way he had shown that he had not slept, while not asking anything critical. It is in this idiotic grey zone between morning coffee and lunch that this kind of thing takes place on many boards here. I see the problem of poor-quality boards in Switzerland as extremely damaging for industry.

It does not need a company to be family-owned and run for atrophy of the chairman and the board of directors to set in. There are a number of other Swiss companies that are not family firms where the excessively long chairmanship of one person has led to problems or will lead to problems. But it is true that family involvement often leads to this problem of hanging around long after the last curtain call. This was certainly the case with Oerlikon-Buehrle. But essentially this problem is a psychological one.

If someone says to you at the age of 35: 'Here's the money, you can travel around the world for three years with your wife', you would probably drop everything and leave immediately. But when you are 70 years old that is a completely different matter. At the start of the life cycle you have so many wonderful plans and projects that you want to realise and achieve: you want to put together an art collection, you want to discover the world. But as the life cycle is approaching its end and retirement looms, it is absolutely perverse to expect someone to look forward to it. The chairmen who can't let go are people who do not want to die. They are desperately looking for some way of staying in the middle of the life cycle and of not slipping towards the end. I once asked the chairman of a major Swiss company when he planned to retire and added that I felt nine out of ten successful men ruined their careers by staying on for too long. But he replied that work was part of human nature and he wanted to stay on as long as possible. A high-profile chairman of a very large company is another example: in every speech he makes he says about every twelve minutes or so how fit he still is. It's ridiculous.

In my case everything is already planned. There has to be another existence outside the job, an existence which one can step into when one has finished one's job. I have that. Also I have learnt to regard my job from a certain self-ironic distance. I still give everything I have, but I cannot identify myself or establish my personal identity through my job. I see all the honours one receives as a chairman or a chief executive, but I know that the moment I step down from the position doors will stop opening automatically for me. Once I am pensioned off nobody will call up and offer me tickets to theatre premières and so on. The ability to step down starts with the realisation that this role you have is only hired out and that when you hang up the chairman's suit you must still find yourself – your own person beneath the suit. One has to be a person, a rounded human being, to be able to survive going into retirement.

Most top managers do not realise this, and do not accept that it is only a role. The great Alfred Schaefer, who built up Union Bank of Switzerland,[7] found it very difficult to let go of the role. As he had to give up his insignia, one after the other, and was confronted with the naked Schaefer, he was unable to face it and fell into a deep depression from which he never emerged. Holzach[8] was exactly the same. Great men. They do what one always hopes employees will do. They identify themselves completely with the job – but then when the job disappears there is suddenly nothing left.

Having said that, I recognise that the role of a director is extremely difficult. I have stepped down from all my directorships, sacrificing considerable financial reward by the way, because I did not feel I could devote the necessary time to the positions. One has to give more than half a day four times a year, otherwise it leads to nothing at all. Hilti in Schaan[9] has recognised the problem and they pay their directors on the understanding that they will spend at least 40 days per year on the company's affairs. A director is then able to understand a company and make a contribution.

Here at Oerlikon I think we have one of the best boards in Switzerland. The basis was good anyway because the current members of the board had been working together previously as a project team when the banks took over in 1990. For five or six months they sat together every weekend, and often during the week, and they really steeped themselves in the business of the group. One concentrated on Bally, another on Balzers (vacuum technology and liquid crystal). When I was asked to join the board for discussions on restructuring they knew more about the company than I did. And they have not forgotten it today. Furthermore they are financially independent and all have their own successful careers. That they are interested in us is a service to mankind; they have no need to work on our board. They are competent and they are under 50. If we want to make an acquisition, they pay very close attention and before they approve it I have to go through a real inquisition, answering very intelligent questions.

Apart from atrophied boards a phenomenon which can lead to problems is undeserved success and that lulls people into a false sense of security. Then when the success disappears there's nothing of substance left. For Oerlikon the money earned in the 1970s through weapons came too easily; the money was there and nothing meaningful was done with it. Added to that there was no financial control at all. There were no monthly reports. There were reports at times during the year, and when these were bad they would be accompanied by a statement that the full year would be better. When, towards the end of the year, it became clear how bad the year was going to be everyone looked to the new budget for the next year to raise their spirits. And then there were the five-year plans which were even rosier – according to them Oerlikon would have an annual turnover of 10 billion francs by now. But I never complained about the way things were done at Oerlikon. My message was only that the company could be improved.

Notes

1. The PC-XII is the latest all-purpose freight or passenger aircraft built by Pilatus Flugzeugwerke, a unit of the Oerlikon-Buehrle group. Pilatus is based in Stans, a small town near Lucerne.

2. Nestlé headquarters are located in the western Swiss town of Vevey.

3. The Rieter and Saurer groups are Switzerland's largest producers of textile machinery. Saurer is the world's largest textile machinery producer.

4. Bernina Naehmaschinen, a sewing machine producer, is based in Steckborn.

5. The Swiss federal government reported a budget deficit of some eight billion Swiss francs for the 1993 financial year. It is projecting a shortfall of at least seven billion francs for 1994. In the second half of the 1980s the Swiss had become used to large budget surpluses.

6. The telecommunications group Ascom Holding AG reported heavy losses in 1992 and even worse losses for 1993. The Swiss market for telecommunications equipment was opened to foreign competition in 1992 and Ascom's lack of competitiveness was quickly exposed.

7. Alfred Schaefer, chairman of the board at UBS, 1964–76.

8. Robert Holzach, chairman of the board at UBS, 1980–88.

9. Hilti AG is Liechtenstein's largest company. It produces materials and tools for use in the construction industry.

Chapter 5

SWITZERLAND AND THE GYPSIES

In the Middle Ages the practice in some parts of Switzerland was to cut an ear off any loitering gypsies before chasing them out of the canton to ensure that if they ever returned they would be spotted immediately and could be punished even more severely.[1] By the twentieth century the treatment of Swiss gypsies, known as the Jenisch people, had improved little.

Between 1926 and 1973 Swiss authorities sanctioned the systematic kidnapping of over 700 Jenisch children by a private children's charity group called Pro-Juventute. The charity group organised a project called *Kinder der Landstrasse* (Children of the Road) aimed at eradicating vagrancy and giving Jenisch children a more stable upbringing than they would have with gypsy parents in caravans on the road. After confiscation parents were prevented from seeing their children until they were of age and, even then, separated families were not told of each other's whereabouts. The children, whose lives were controlled by their guardians at Pro-Juventute, usually endured a merry-go-round of foster parents, orphanages and, if they became difficult or criminal, borstals and gaols.

The Jenisch claim that the aim of the *Kinder der Landstrasse* project was the extermination of the Jenisch people, and comments by the organisers and others associated with it seem to back this up. Alfred Siegfried, the founder and for many years the head of the project, wrote: 'We must say that we have already achieved much if these people do not start a family, do not reproduce without restraint and bring new generations of degenerate and abnormal children into the world.' And in a Zurich University dissertation in 1944 on how to deal with the problem of tramps and road travellers, a Swiss lawyer wrote: 'From a eugenic and criminal point of view we would therefore favour the sterilisation of some seriously ill road traveller types.'[2]

The Jenisch people exist throughout Europe but are concentrated in Switzerland. They are believed to be descended from road travellers and European gypsies who decided to stay in Switzerland during the seventeenth and eighteenth centuries. The Jenisch speak their own language, and they are now fighting for official recognition as a minority people in Switzerland and for the preservation of their language and culture.

Kinder der Landstrasse was exposed by a Swiss magazine in 1973 and abandoned after a wave of public outrage. Pro-Juventute has tried to make amends; it has formally apologised to the Jenisch people and in 1982 it gave them access to its files on the kidnapped children to facilitate family reunions.[3] In 1986 the Swiss president Alphons Egli also apologised to the Jenisch people and in 1992 the Swiss government awarded a total of 7.5 million Swiss francs ($5.3 million) to a number of Jenisch families in compensation.

Some 5,000 of Switzerland's estimated 35,000 Jenisch people take to the road every summer. They are mostly antique dealers or scrap merchants and use their trips to drum up business. The remainder have integrated into Swiss society. The travelling minority disparagingly refer to the integrated as the 'cement Jenisch' or the 'settled ones'. The Swiss government has provided the Jenisch people with caravan parks for their sole use all over Switzerland, and Swiss schools are willing to offer Jenisch children correspondence courses for the summer months that they spend travelling with their parents.

In this chapter Mariella Mehr, a Jenisch woman who was one of the kidnapped children under the *Kinder der Landstrasse* project, describes her personal experiences.

Notes

1. Haesler (1967), p. 29.

2. Quoted in appendix to Mehr (1981), p. 190.

3. Pro-Juventute today makes no attempt to justify the *Kinder der Landstrasse* project. Karl Gruber, a spokesman for the group, told the author in June 1992: 'At that time the project reflected thinking that was widespread among the Swiss people. There was a fundamental belief that minority groups should be integrated into the strait-jacket of one culture and society.' He added: 'Gypsies had a poor reputation and were regarded as thieves.' He added that some of the motivation for the project also came from racial views similar to those held by the Nazi regime in Germany in the 1930s and 1940s, where gypsies were imprisoned in concentration camps and systematically killed. 'Unfortunately, thinking of this sort also crosses borders.'

KINDER DER LANDSTRASSE

Mariella Mehr

The postmaster at the corner post office in the small mountain village of Tomils in the south-eastern canton of Graubuenden nods his head vigorously in recognition. She lives in the yellow house just down the road, the 'gypsy house' as the children playing in the street call it. Mariella Mehr, 47 years old, is waiting at the bead-curtained doorstep in a pale orange silk top and trousers and loose sandals. 'I have always liked silk,' she says later. She is very short-sighted, blind in her left eye and sees little with her right eye but still manages to read and write with the help of aids.

Mehr is a successful author and has published a number of books and plays. 'I began writing poems in the homes when I was 12 years old because I had nobody to tell my feelings to. One of the notes in the files on me said that I seemed to believe I was a poet but added that I certainly was not one.'

She bends her head through a low doorway into a small room with chairs and table and many sandstone sculptures. A lolling dog and a cat keep her company. 'I came here to find out why my people lived in this part of Switzerland many years ago and to write about them.'

My people moved here with their caravans at the start of the eighteenth century. They were horse dealers and apparently felt comfortable here. They came from Austria, through the Tyrol, to this area. That was what interested me and is why I moved here five years ago. I wanted to find out why they had lived here and what had made them stay. This is also the area where a lot of the psychologists who researched my people from top to bottom live.

I also moved here to write a book about my people. The book

110

I have written is a sardonic story about how Zeus comes down from Olympus to rid himself of his immortality and chooses a psychiatric clinic for this purpose – the Waldhaus Chur clinic which I know very well. The doctors and professors at that clinic have spent decades dealing with my people.

I discovered later that I was snatched away from my mother at birth. We were both still in hospital. I learnt Jenisch in the homes and education institutes. At times up to 50 per cent of the children in the orphanages were Jenisch and so we taught each other to speak Jenisch. It was also a secret language against the nuns; the homes were then mostly run by nuns. There were also other orphans in the homes and during the early years of my childhood these included refugee orphans from Germany and other countries who had lost their parents in the War and in the concentration camps, and some children from poor Swiss families who in the economic hardship after the War were simply not able to feed their children and therefore handed them over to social care. We Jenisch were in the homes because of a programme to destroy the Jenisch way of life in Switzerland and forcibly to integrate the Jenisch people into society.

For a long time I was totally unaware of what was being done to the Jenisch people. When I once asked an official at Pro-Juventute who my parents were, he said: 'You don't need to worry about that. Your mother was a slut and your father was an alcoholic.' And that was the general tone in which Pro-Juventute referred to the parents of all Jenisch children they had kidnapped. It helped stop the children from trying to find and return to their parents because nobody particularly wants to go back to a slut and an alcoholic.

Of course, we children believed that our parents were simply too poor to look after us and had given us away. It made it easier for us to accept that we had no contact with our parents. None of us would ever have imagined that there was a system behind the separation from our parents. I don't think it would have been possible for a child to live with the knowledge that it had been kidnapped from its parents.

I first realised that there was a system behind the kidnappings when I was 18 and in detention for trying to marry a gypsy I loved. You could be locked up for that. My guardian at Pro-Juventute recommended to the government of the canton of

Graubuenden that I be locked up to prevent me marrying a gypsy and the government approved it. My son was born while I was in detention and I was allowed to keep him for the first 12 months. But then they gave me the choice of handing him over to them or having him forcibly taken from me and serving the full three years of my sentence. I had to hand him over because I realised that I could manage to survive the reduced sentence of 19 months but not the full three years. That was when I realised that the separations were due to racist motives.

From that point on, in the gaol, I began to resist the system. I fought to get my son back. First, after I had had to give him away, he was placed with foster parents. But the foster mother was a fool. She left him next to a tub of very hot water to answer the doorbell and he fell in and was terribly burnt. Christian, my son, had to spend nine months in hospital and then they gave him back to me, more or less a cripple. But they only gave him back because I had finally married. I did not marry Christian's father, but simply a proxy so that I could get my son back and shake off the official guardians.

When I then separated from my husband they took Christian away from me again and placed him in a home as far away from me as possible, in the hope that I would lose contact with him. But before he started school I found him, took him away from the home he was in and brought him back to where I was living in Berne. Soon after two policemen arrived and said they had come to collect Christian. I asked them to wait at the door and went into the kitchen where Christian was, picked up the largest knife I could find and said: 'Okay, if you come in someone is going to get killed. Either you or me.' And since then I have not had any problems. They did not come back, neither Pro-Juventute nor anybody from the government.

I think I managed to survive because I hated. I think I started hating when I was about ten years old, when I first realised that people were trying to hurt me, trying to destroy me and I knew I was fighting against strangers. And this was probably the only reason I was able to survive. If children are badly treated by their parents, or by their brothers and sisters, they always blame themselves because they cannot live with the idea that their parents, whom they love, are maltreating them and do not love them. That is the start of a self-destructive process. I did not blame myself. I knew I was fighting against strangers and did not feel I was being abandoned by people I loved.

I know very little about my parents. My mother was born near this village and spent her first five years in this area. She was one of the first children to be snatched away by Pro-Juventute. It was more or less a kidnapping in the middle of the night. They simply came, saw and grabbed. My father was from southern Switzerland, from the canton of Ticino. He grew up there with foster parents because he had also been snatched away from his Jenisch people, but in his case it was the authorities not Pro-Juventute who kidnapped him. The two of them met by chance, where so many people meet, at the train station in Zurich.

I first met my mother when I was 23 and then it was already too late. I had looked for her; I wanted to know where I had come from, and whether my mother really was a slut. I don't remember how I got hold of her telephone number, but anyway we arranged to meet in her favourite bar, the St Jakob, in Zurich at six o'clock. So there we stood, looking at each other, two complete strangers, and the first words she said were: 'Couldn't you dress a little more feminine?' It was true; I did look more like a boy than a girl. I used to wear trousers, I had silk socks and was very thin then. For my mother it was a shock. She had imagined something completely different of a daughter with a five-year-old child of her own and then she suddenly had this half-boy in front of her. That was really the end of the relationship. My mother died soon after without us seeing each other again.

My parents were separated and had lost touch with each other so I looked for my father next. But the meeting with him was even worse. I looked for him via dozens of different institutions in Zurich and then at some point I managed to find out where his favourite bar was. I went to the bar with a friend because I did not have the courage to go on my own and I remember the barkeeper, who was a very old woman, coming to our table in those awful grey woven slippers that so many people used to wear indoors then. I was very shy and asked in a small voice if she knew a Mr So and So, and told her the name of my father. She raised her stick which she leant on while walking and shakingly pointed at the table reserved for regular customers and said: 'That one with the big moustache.' He was the loudest one at the table.

My father looked just like the typical gypsy: dark, wiry and an unbelievable drunk. I said to my friend: 'I can't just go over to that table and say, "Hello, I'm your daughter".' And so we drank a beer and waited for him to finish. When he got up to leave I told my friend I would meet him outside and tell him who I was there. It was freezing cold and I was standing in the snow and slush on the pavement – the shoes that I had polished especially to try and make a good impression were a mess.

He came out and looked me up and down, the way men do, and then said: 'Well girl, how much do you cost?' And I swallowed and very shyly told him I was his daughter. 'You will have to prove that first,' he said. So I dug in my pocket for my purse and took out my identity card and gave it to him. Immediately he burst into tears and in the freezing cold spent 20 minutes crying and telling me how he had never wanted to abandon my mother and that he would support me financially from now on, and that he had always hoped I would return and so on. Finally he asked whether I wouldn't like to have a drink with him. So we went back inside and he shouted and told the whole room that I was his daughter. We drank a few rounds and then this relationship was also at an end. I never saw him again. I didn't want to see him again. As far as I know he disappeared.

I don't feel myself to be Swiss. I avoid as much as possible speaking Swiss-German dialect; I prefer to speak German because that is the language I write in. I can also speak Jenisch and Romany, but unfortunately I cannot write in those languages. I can't think of any reason why I should feel myself to be Swiss; there is nothing that binds me to Switzerland. But I don't know whether I feel myself to be Jenisch either. It's difficult if you have not grown up as a Jenisch in a caravan. It is certainly true that if I had grown up as a Jenisch I would not have learnt German well enough to start writing it and I would not have become an author. This internal turmoil that I feel is not peculiar to the Jenisch, other people have it as well. I only know that when I am together with Jenisch people, particularly those who are travelling, I feel very comfortable with them and I enjoy sitting around their fires.

Of course part of the reason for my ambiguous feelings about where I belong is due to my profession and to my own private development as a person which have made me an outsider: I don't need to belong to a group, be it Swiss or Jenisch. But it is also because I do not have a feeling of home. I don't know whether this is good or bad – it's certainly no problem for me. My child-hood was not spent in one place. With the exception of one period of nearly four years I never spent more than one year in any one place. There are countrysides I remember and people I remember, but there's nothing that could trigger homesickness or the feeling of it being home in me. This does not mean that I cannot develop intensive relationships with people and places, but that is an adult emotion. There are thousands of pictures I have in my mind from my childhood, but there are no feelings connected with places where I could say: 'I won't to go back there.'

I don't feel that travelling is what distinguishes the Jenisch people, as some Jenisch claim. The Jenisch people and the gypsies in general divide the world into the travellers and the settled people. But I don't think travel is a matter of location and not putting down roots. I travel all the time even though I have now lived in this house for five years. Anyway the travelling is a tradition born out of necessity. The gypsies, all gypsy peoples, were once settled as well being originally a caste in India. They were smiths who mostly made weapons and following the collapse of the Indian kingdoms around 1,500 years ago they lost the economic basis for their exist-ence. So they had to look for a means of survival; they tried various other trades and at the same time began migrating overland from India towards the West. Eventually they arrived in Europe.

Since the travelling arose out of economic necessity I don't see why I should integrate this into my consciousness as a Jenisch person. The Sinti in Germany have completely abandoned this myth of the travelling and that is correct. They say they have their religion, their tradition, their culture and so on, but the travelling was only a fringe matter which was due to economic necessity and later, during the Third Reich, to racial persecution. And when I see the caravans of Jenisch people here in Switzerland I often think that there is nothing more bourgeois than one of those caravans.

There is certainly a Jenisch character, a kind of 'Jenischness'. You can see it in the religion, although there are very few Jenisch who will speak with you about religion – that's rather a taboo subject. You can also see it in the language and in the relationship the Jenisch have to property and the ability to let go of property. I, for example, am very happy in this house; it's 300 years old and I like the atmosphere. But I would have no difficulty in leaving it at a day's notice if necessary. I suppose it is really a feeling that I own more and different things compared with what average people feel they own.

There is certainly a considerable amount of the Jenisch culture that could be preserved with support from the Swiss government. The language is an obvious example. There are about 38,000 people in Switzerland who speak Romansch,[1] which is recognised as a minority language here. There are around the same number of Jenisch in Switzerland, but the Jenisch language is not recognised. Then there is, as for all tribal cultures in Africa and Asia, the Jenisch handicraft. There are also things in religion and medicine that could be saved with support. But the danger, and that is why I tend to be cautious in this area, is that this could all turn into some kind of folklore. What we don't want is for Jenisch people to start dressing themselves up like Jenisch people a century ago and to start selling that as Jenisch culture.

I always say that the light skin colour of the Jenisch people is actually a great misfortune. Because you cannot distinguish the Jenisch people from other people in Switzerland by appearance, it is very easy for the Jenisch to assimilate into Swiss society. We have never had to stand up for our rights as a group. Some of the other gypsy peoples in Europe are much darker-skinned and they don't assimilate as well. But the Jenisch people have learnt perfectly how to assimilate and have almost disappeared into Swiss society.

One of the reasons that I have started talking and writing openly about my experiences is to try and ensure that future generations of Jenisch or other travelling people do not suffer the same fate as we did. For a long time I did not see the importance of this. I was too involved in dealing with my own experiences – in accepting who I was, where I had come from and what I had experienced. But now I think it's very important to let everyone know what happened.

When the persecution of the Jenisch stopped we were given the right to look at the individual files they had kept on us at Pro-Juventute. I had the right to see a huge number of files, probably 100,000 pages, because there were files on my father and mother and also on my brother. My brother hanged himself when he was 12 in the attic of a home in Bremgarten for psychologically disturbed children; he would be 50 years old now.

I asked my lawyer to demand copies of the files I had a right to see and because they were too lazy to photocopy them they sent me the originals of what I wanted. Now I have them and I am going to keep them. I do not intend to return them, although I don't really know what I am going to do with them. But I think I am an exception among the Jenisch people. The majority have not asked to see their files. Most of them were afraid, and I can understand why. It is painful and difficult to deal with your own history when you have had the idea so deeply drummed into you that what happened to you and your people is all your fault, and is because of the failings of your people. It is in the psychological reports and notes that are in many of the files, comments like 'congenitally afflicted', 'feelings of inferiority' and so on.

I read my files. There were about 15,000 pages that covered me alone. One of the comments in there from a psychological report on me in 1964 when I was 17 years old read: 'This is a congenitally afflicted, neurotic person with psychopathic tendencies. A permanent committal to a psychological clinic cannot be excluded.' There were other similar comments. It was very difficult to read things like that and it led to a real identity crisis for me. I went to Spain for a year and wrote a book about bullfighting to try and avoid dealing with the whole problem. But then I came back and said to myself that I had had long enough to come to terms with the problem and so I read through all the files, those of my family as well. Then I wrote a play, called *Kinder der Landstrasse*, which deals with one phase of my life when I was in gaol.

In a way my son has suffered even more than I have because he is dark-skinned and because he has Jewish features. He has the features of his father. He is addicted to drugs. He sees his background and his origins as a burden, only as a burden. Because he can't hide himself, he can't assimilate the way most Jenisch people have. It's the problem I mentioned before. Most of the Jenisch people can hide because they are pale-skinned, but he cannot. And he wishes he could hide. Among a group of Swiss he stands out, looking obviously foreign even though he's not. He is finding things very difficult and I just pray that one day he will come across one of the gypsy peoples, and they will take him in and make him realise that he is one of them.

Note

1. Rhaeto-Roman, or Romansch, is Switzerland's fourth national language and is spoken mainly in the canton of Graubuenden.

Chapter 6

THE SWISS ARMY

The army is central to Switzerland. For many it is a sacred icon that represents the core of Swiss national identity, history and society. It looks back on a mercenary tradition in the Middle Ages when Swiss infantry were the most feared in Europe. The Swiss army prides itself on having deterred a Nazi invasion of Switzerland during the Second World War and on having safeguarded Swiss neutrality for almost 150 years. No Swiss man can ignore the army for he must spend the better part of his adult life with a military uniform in his cupboard and a rifle with live ammunition in his cellar.

Critics of the army also exist, however. They argue the army is bad for Swiss society by creating an opaque *Maennerbund* (men's association) élite that dominates both the military and civilian establishments.[1] Nazi forces never invaded Switzerland, they say, because the Swiss compromised their neutrality sufficiently with Germany to make invasion unnecessary for Hitler. In the post-Cold War world, they maintain, the Swiss army is an anachronism, which should be replaced by social service or civil aid duty.

In the 1980s some of these critics collected the necessary signatures to force a national referendum on whether to abolish the Swiss army. Although the proposal was rejected, an astonishing third of the votes was in favour of disbanding the military. The referendum shook Switzerland, amazed neighbouring countries and accelerated the pace of reforms planned for the Swiss military.

Iconoclasm often provokes angry reactions and the public discussion over the army, which later spread to its choice of armaments, is among the bitterest debates to divide Swiss society since the Second World War.

Critics of the military may raise hackles in the Swiss establishment, but traitors are not tolerated and are crucified. In June 1977 Jean-Louis Jeanmaire, a brigadier-general commanding Switzerland's air defences from 1969 to 1975, was sentenced to 18 years in gaol for passing classified military documents to the Soviet Union. When the news of his arrest broke, the country was outraged. The tabloid press, given the lead by the justice minister, Kurt Furgler,

who in parliament condemned the 'treasonable' activities of a man
who had yet to be proven guilty, branded Jeanmaire 'the traitor of
the century'. Jeanmaire's wife, who was also accused but then later
exonerated when the court dismissed the charges against her, suffered a stroke under the strain and died before her husband was
released from prison.

Years later, while Jeanmaire was still serving his sentence, questions began to be asked. Officials involved in the case admitted the
evidence had been weak and had not justified the severity of the
sentence. Two former parliamentarians set up a commission to
press for an appeal to be heard. Jeanmaire was released early in
1988 and immediately began work to overturn his conviction. He
claimed he had been made a scapegoat for alleged Swiss leaks of
US technological secrets to the East in the 1970s. The United States
was particularly furious about the leak of technological details on
an aircraft early warning system and was threatening to class
Switzerland as a similar security risk to communist countries as
far as technological exports were concerned. The Swiss authorities
needed to present a high-profile conviction to show they had
plugged the hole. Jeanmaire died unvindicated in January 1992. At
the time of his death he was preparing the third submission for his
case to be reopened. The first two were rejected.

In this chapter in one of the last interviews he gave before his
death, Jeanmaire defends himself against his conviction. Andreas
Gross, a member of parliament for the Social Democratic Party
and a founder member of the movement for the abolition of the
Swiss army, criticises the military and explains why it is redundant.
The case for the army is presented by chief of staff General Arthur
Liener, one the country's highest-ranking peacetime military of-
ficers.

Note

1. A recent study which polled 150 personnel managers of major Swiss
companies and of administration in the public sector discovered that although
there was now more concern at the cost of having senior managers away several
weeks a year on officer training courses than in the early 1980s, when a similar
poll was held, the vast majority still regarded military officer experience as a
very important asset when appointing new staff (*Schweizerische Arbeitgeber-
Zeitung*, 3, 20 January 1994, p. 65).

THE TRAITOR

Jean-Louis Jeanmaire

The taxi driver recognises the address immediately. He was a sergeant in the army and once served under Jeanmaire: 'He talks to everyone about his case, anyone he can find. Maybe the sentence was harsh, but if the positions had been reversed he would have shown no mercy to a subordinate who had done something similar.'

Jeanmaire is waiting at the door to his flat and after the greetings leads the way into a small lounge where he sits behind a small table, almost like a field commander at a table of maps. The table is covered with documents and files, with a magnifying glass to hand. Piled on the floor and bookshelves of the room are many more files and sheaves of papers. Jeanmaire is a stocky, balding man with white hair, a pot belly and an elfish smile. He has thick, bushy eyebrows and hearing aids in both ears. Occasionally he clenches his fist and pounds the table to drive home a point; at other times he wags a thick finger warningly in the air. He often looks at his documents and now and then marks something that has caught his eye with a pen. During some pauses he snaps the braces he is wearing. A medallion hangs from a leather cord around his neck. He has prepared a list of topics he wants to cover in the conversation and he goes through them with determination, much as the chairman of a committee might adhere to an agenda. During the conversation he interrupts himself and says he must put the potatoes on to boil: 'I'll need something to eat tonight.' He wears horn-rimmed glasses but takes them off frequently and swings them in one hand by the frame.

I was framed! They claimed I had passed over secrets on a tank project, but I kept on telling them I had nothing to do with the tanks. I was in the anti-aircraft defence. I had no access to information about tanks and US weapon systems. And I never saw anything to do with the Florida system.

I first met Denissenko in 1959. Almost the first words I said to him were that I hated the communists. He replied that the communists of today were different from the Bolsheviks. My wife was born in Russia and that gave us something to talk about. Her father had been working there before the Bolshevik Revolution but once the Bolsheviks came to power the family was expelled. Denissenko and I became friends. I liked meeting him and talking to him about the Soviet Union and Tsarist Russia. He seemed like an officer in the old Tsarist tradition.

Contacts with the Soviets were not a problem. We were allowed to have contacts with foreign military attachés as long as we reported them to the army protocol department. I was the only officer who reported every meeting I had with Denissenko. There were other officers who met military attachés or other diplomats from Eastern European countries and did not report every meeting. I met Denissenko publicly in a restaurant once. I wouldn't have done that if I had had something to hide. I remember that during the meal in the restaurant with Denissenko and our wives I went to the toilet and on the way passed the restaurant owner. I pointed out Denissenko to him, saying: 'That is the Russian military attaché from Berne.' I was not hiding anything, I was not a traitor.

The only military information I gave him was a copy of the Swiss army's mobilisation plan. And, since the authorities could not find anything else, that was what they got me on. The plan was classified as secret, but that was wrong – a mistake – it should not have been classified. It was of no military value; it had been formulated in 1947 and today it is no longer classified. I mean, there were over 10,000 copies of this plan distributed among various officers and officials and so on in Switzerland. It simply was not a particularly secret or valuable document.

We were on the balcony of my apartment in Lausanne, Denissenko and I, when I gave it to him. 'It's nothing more than a cookery book,' I told him as I handed it to him. I gave it to him out of friendship, because he was a nice person, not because I had evil aims or because I wanted to harm my country. I also gave him a list of Swiss army officers and I later thought that might have been a mistake. But not the mobilisation plan, that simply was not sensitive. Every year the Swiss army invited all the foreign military attachés stationed in Berne to a military demonstration and they were given information about Swiss mobilisation there.

Perhaps I made a mistake in giving it to him. But the Soviet Union would have had its own operations plan for military conflict in western Europe and the Atlantic. They would not have been very interested in a battle in Switzerland. And by giving him a copy of the plan I actually helped to deter the Russians: if a Russian general knew that the moment he attacked Switzerland 650,000 armed men would shoot out of the ground like asparagus then he would have thought twice before attacking. In a few hours, 650,000 armed men![1]

Later, much later, I discovered that my wife had been having an affair with Denissenko behind my back. While I was in gaol Marie-Louise came to visit me and confessed to having had a relationship with Denissenko. I covered her hands with my hands and told her to stop. 'We won't talk about it,' I said. I couldn't blame her, I was often away. Where would the world be if one did not tolerate occasional flings? Denissenko was a nice man and an attractive man. If we had been at war I do not think I could have shot at him in anger. It shows you that friendship knows no borders and no ideologies.

Denissenko left Berne in 1964. The last time I saw him was on 30 May in that year. He was posted back to Moscow I think, but I am not sure. We have not had any contact since. He has not contacted me either. It wasn't possible before. Now, with Gorbachev in power, it might be but I won't believe in *perestroika* until they take Lenin's body out of the mausoleum.

I had really forgotten all about him and was preparing myself for a well-earned retirement when the madness started. From the end of August 1975 I was put under surveillance. I did not realise it at the time but afterwards it was obvious. The army had asked me to put together a study on civil defence in foreign countries instead of allowing me to retire, which I was due to do. It was something that no one really needed or was interested in. Now I can see that it was really a trap to keep me in an office in the military department where they could keep an eye on me and where they hoped I would do something that would give them proof that I was the traitor they were looking for.

Then almost a year later I was arrested. It was on 9 August

1976 in Lausanne on my way to the train station at 06.55 in the morning. A couple of police officers jumped out of a police car as I walked past, threw me into the car and drove me to Berne. They could have arrested me in a more civilised manner in my office – they did not have to make such a dramatic scene of it all - they knew I was coming to the office and they knew I was not going to escape. And ten minutes after arresting me they were in our flat, scaring my wife out of her wits and tearing the apartment apart.

For the first three days they left my cell door open because they were afraid I might commit suicide. After two months in gaol my arrest became public knowledge. Justice minister Kurt Furgler told parliament and in his speech on 7 October 1976, which was before I had been tried and before a court had decided whether I was guilty or not, used the word 'treason' in connection with me 13 times. After his speech I became the 'traitor of the century' and the insurance company, which owned the flat my wife and I had been living in, gave notice on the contract and demanded I move out.

It makes you ask yourself, as it has made me ask myself, what treason is. During the War the Swiss army shot 17 men dead for treason between 1942 and 1944. What I did was not treason! At most I made a mistake, a failure of discipline, but it was not treason.

At first they kept me in solitary confinement for 313 days; later I was held in a cell of 5.8 square metres for 22 months during the investigation and trial. For the whole 12 years of my time in prison I never had warm water and I was not allowed paper to write on until January 1978. The army even ordered that there was to be no contact between me and other officers. I could not even receive former army friends as visitors while I was in gaol. I discovered in gaol that there is a great difference between loneliness and being alone. It was the being alone that caused me a lot of suffering. But I was never lonely. I received a lot of letters. And I never cried.

But I was always planning an appeal to overturn the verdict against me. I rejected their offer of release in return for silence when I was in prison because that would have prevented me from telling the truth once I got out. As I lived on and did not die, the situation became awkward for them; they had hoped I would die in prison. I have done nothing that harmed Switzerland. I have been through my case and there are 142 instances of abuse of office that they are guilty of in their treatment of me. I am now working through the documents for the appeal.

If you sentence a man who is 67 years old to 18 years in gaol then you are pretty sure he won't come back – it's a death sentence. But I came back. And I *will* have the last word!

[*Author's note*: Following this interview, in late 1991, Jeanmaire travelled to Moscow to visit Denissenko with a Swiss television crew. The first meeting between the two men for almost 30 years was filmed. Denissenko, formally dressed and living in a modest home, seemed both bemused and slightly embarrassed by the visit, while Jeanmaire appeared nervous.

They talked on a bench in a Moscow park. Jeanmaire forgave Denissenko for his affair with Marie-Louise. 'No, something came out, unfortunately, Marie-Louise kept a small diary. It came out while I was in gaol, I was informed that you and she met together – there was a huge story. In any case, when I found out the first thing that I did was to write to Marie-Louise from the gaol: "Don't worry, I forgive you." And I forgive you as well. It went so far that federal president Gnaeggi found it necessary to say that Mr Denissenko and my wife occasionally met behind my back.'

Denissenko told Jeanmaire he had heard that Jeanmaire had been punished for giving him important documents. But, he said emphatically, he never received any documents from Jeanmaire. For a moment Jeanmaire looked shamefaced. 'I can only explain this with the fact that when I was in solitary confinement and so on I said things that were not true. And I never came back to correct them later.'[2]

Jeanmaire died four months later in Berne.]

Notes

1. In the 1960s the Swiss army had a fully mobilised strength of around 650,000 men. All Swiss men were required to perform military service until the age of 52 and, when not actually in the army, kept their uniforms and weapons with live ammunition at home so that if a rapid mobilisation was necessary they could go straight to their stations. Military service has since been reduced to the age of 42.

2. Jeanmaire and Denissenko spoke to the Swiss television news programme *10 vor 10* on 8 October 1991 (courtesy of Schweizer Fernsehen DRS).

THE CRITIC

Andreas Gross

Andreas Gross, 42, speaks in his home – a small cottage near a noisily flowing stream on the outskirts of Zurich. The house has low ceilings and is filled with light pine furniture. There are piles of papers and books everywhere. Gross has long bushy black hair and sports a full beard. He is wearing an open shirt and jeans. In the kitchen his mother-in-law stands ironing. He introduces her while edging past the ironing board and entering the lounge.

Gross helped finance his university studies in Zurich with work as a journalist for a motor racing magazine. 'I was also the Formula Two motor racing correspondent in Europe for a number of Swiss newspapers. I particularly enjoyed being in England. It is the cradle of motor racing. In England the motor racing circuits have the most atmosphere. I lived in Zurich but used to travel around Europe to the races in an old Volkswagen beetle and occasionally I would have to drive all through the night on my way to or from a race.'

He joined the Swiss Social Democratic Party in 1974. From 1979 to 1983 he served as chairman of the Young Socialists, the independent youth movement of the Social Democrats. Gross's main interest is in direct democracy. At university he wrote a dissertation on the first initiative in Switzerland inspired by the labour movement in 1894 which called for the right to work. The proposal failed to win approval in the ensuing national referendum partly because it was rejected by working-class voters in the cities. 'This showed me the great gap between the potential of direct democracy and the realisation of this potential.' Gross runs a private academic research institute for direct democracy and also lectures on the subject at two German universities.

I became interested in the army through my grandfather. He was a liberal entrepreneur in Basle who owned an engineering factory. When I was young, about nine years old or so, he began having discussions with me about all kinds of topics and this went on throughout my adolescence. But in particular we talked about politics and the military; we talked about Kennedy and Nixon, and also about Vietnam. Though he was fond and proud of the army and of his military career, I later became a pacifist. But I learnt from him how important discussion is and also how to discuss.

When I grew up, but was still a young man, I was alone and was not strong enough to refuse military service and go to prison for my views. There was no alternative to military service in Switzerland at that time and I went to the recruits' school like all men my age. But I had a very anti-military attitude, a pacifist attitude. I made it quite clear immediately how absurd I thought the whole business was.

I was sent to Ticino and was trained to fire artillery guns that were so old they dated from before the First World War – and this was in 1972! The joke among the recruits was that if we ever had to shoot those cannons in anger we wouldn't have a chance of hitting anything, but we could be quite sure the enemy would know where we were and that we really would be in danger. I continued with military service until 1982 but it became increasingly difficult for me and I developed stomach pains and became unable to sleep. And then in 1982 I simply said I had had enough. I couldn't take it any longer. I was suffering psychological and physical ill health as a result of military service and I was no longer prepared to continue with the absurdity. I was glad to go and the military was glad that I went – the satisfaction over my departure was mutual. They knew I was president of the Young Socialists and were glad to be rid of a troublemaker. Officially I was declared psychologically unfit for military service, but in fact it was an agreement on both sides that I should leave.

Today the majority of people who avoid military service use this option – the so-called 'blauer Weg' (the blue path). In the end this is just a big lie. Rather than changing the law in recognition of the fact that no one wants to do military service they allow over 10,000 people to avoid military service on so-called medical grounds.[1] In my case I simply provided a medical certificate stating that the stomach complaints I had were due to psychological stress.

For the army there is always the risk that if they force someone to stay against doctors' orders and something happens to that person, the army would have to pay compensation rather than the insurance company.

But I cannot stand civil defence service and the lunacy that goes on there every day either. Now in Switzerland once you have completed military service you still have to do civil defence. Civil defence is the whole nuclear fall-out shelter business. Civil defence is not social service – it's just as military as the military service.[2] On three separate occasions, from 1985 to 1990, I did civil defence service instead of military service. Each of those experiences made it quite clear to me that Switzerland's civil defence is still locked into the Cold War thinking of the possibility of an atomic war. My conscience could not accept this and I was convinced this was wrong, and so I refused to continue with civil defence service as well. So I was hauled before a court and after three separate proceedings in the summer of 1993 I was sentenced to 45 days' *Halbgefangenschaft* (semi-imprisonment).[3]

That is the story of my long battle with the Swiss army. But there is still the story of why the Swiss army is redundant and why I, together with others, have tried to have it abolished.

One of the most common arguments supporters of the Swiss army and of military service have for its existence is that military service contributes to the democratic stability and consensus of Swiss society. The argument claims that the army allows you to meet people from other classes, both rich and poor – bank executives serving alongside factory workers. But this is a myth. It is an attempt to legitimise and justify military service and the existence of the army. You do not need a military service, or an army, to allow people from different classes to make contact with each other. Apart from anything else, during my military service in the artillery there was a high proportion of students so that in fact I did not meet anyone from other classes, I simply met the same people I spent time with outside military service.

It is also a myth to say that the stability and the consensus of Swiss politics is due to the classlessness of the Swiss army where people of all walks of life meet and march up and down mountains together. This argument completely underestimates the ability of the Swiss people to maintain their own national and political identity. Not long ago I read this argument once again, that if the army

was abolished Switzerland would disintegrate. It is insulting to the
Swiss people. Switzerland's democratic system, its political culture
in which everyone feels that he or she has the right to participate
in the democratic process and can contribute something, binds us
together much more than military service and the army does.

The political culture is what keeps the Swiss together despite
the linguistic and cultural differences that have often led to tension
between the German-, French- and Italian-speaking parts of the
country. It is the political culture of direct democracy that distinguishes a banker from Geneva from a banker from Lyon, an
insurance salesman from Zurich from one in Munich or Vienna,
and a taxi driver in Lugano from one in Milan. Of course there
are differences between French-speaking and German-speaking
Switzerland but, even with this gap, what binds us together is the
role and rights of the citizen in Swiss society which are very
different from the role or rights a citizen has in Germany, or in
France, or in Austria, or in Italy. It is true that each of the three
main cultures and language groups in Switzerland is very much
influenced by the three neighbouring countries whose language it
speaks. German television is much watched in German-speaking
Switzerland, French television is watched in Francophone Switzerland and Italian television in the south. In German Switzerland
many people are well-informed about politics in Germany, while
in west Switzerland hardly anyone knows the names of German
politicians but is, on the other hand, well-versed in French politics.

This is what makes Switzerland modern and progressive in
Europe, ahead of other European countries. The reason three cultures are so well integrated here is because of direct democracy
and the decentralised federal structure, because each individual feels
he or she can contribute to and shape the political discussion.
Direct democracy is not an obstruction to Swiss membership of
the European Union; in fact it could be of benefit to Europe because it could force people in Europe to think about democracy.
Direct democracy forces politicians to persuade the people. Without
direct democracy politicians can command the people and do not
need to persuade them. It's crucial to convince the Swiss people
that they have something to offer Europe rather than have them
thinking they must choose between direct democracy and membership of the European Union.

These ties between Switzerland's three cultural and language groups and the countries of their mother languages has helped maintain Swiss neutrality. It would have been too dangerous for Switzerland to take sides in European conflicts because it would almost certainly have forced one of the language groups to choose between Switzerland and the country of its language. If Switzerland had not been neutral the country would probably have joined World War One and disintegrated.[4]

Swiss neutrality gives Switzerland a special role, a special responsibility in Europe today. The history and tradition of neutrality which really started with the Congress of Vienna in 1815[5] allows Switzerland to offer an alternative security policy of demilitarisation as a model for other countries in Europe.

The *Gruppe fuer eine Schweiz ohne Armee* (Group for a Switzerland without an army) developed from this kind of fundamental idea. For me personally it was something that had been developing in my mind for some time. But the decision by myself and around a hundred other people who were members of the Young Socialists to found the movement was finally triggered by the NATO two-track decision in the second half of the 1970s and the US plans for a neutron bomb. These policies made the craziness of military policy based on nuclear arms and strategic plans for a possible war in Europe clear. It was obvious that any war between East and West in Europe would have escalated into a nuclear war and that nobody would have survived such a conflict. It was simply senseless. Instead of preparing for something you can't survive you should try to prevent it happening.

In Switzerland the army was not, and is still not, armed with nuclear weapons. There was a bitter debate in Switzerland in the 1960s over whether the army should become nuclear or not, and in the end the Swiss government decided of its own accord in 1966 to propose a nuclear-free army and this was approved by parliament.[6] This makes the whole discussion of disarmament and demilitarisation in Switzerland very different from the one in Germany or in Britain. Because we are free of nuclear weapons and because we are a small state that does not represent a threat for any other state we have more room for manoeuvre and can develop in other directions.

These ideas led us, at the Young Socialists, to the conclusion that Switzerland could and should abolish its army. We also thought then and we still think now that this would help change

Switzerland domestically because the Swiss army is a superfluous national institution which shapes the thinking of the Swiss people into a very militaristic mould. In the twentieth century, with the exception of anti-aircraft activity during the Second World War, the Swiss army has only been deployed against the country's own people, for example during the General Strike of 1918.[7]

The GSoA is a success story. It was founded in 1982 by a hundred people and is now a movement with some 30,000 members. Together with the feminist movement and the ecological movement, it is one of the big social and political movements of Switzerland. The fact that 36 per cent voted for the abolition of the Swiss army in 1989 cannot be ignored and was a great success. It changed the culture in Switzerland and made it legitimate to criticise the army on a fundamental level. Previously criticism of the army was not tolerated. The military and the establishment saw the F/A-18 vote as a chance for revenge for 1989 and they turned the referendum into another vote on the question of whether Switzerland should have an army or not, rather than just a debate about the sense of having 34 F/A-18s in the air force. We lost the F/A-18 vote but that will not stop us.[8]

Our objective remains a Switzerland without an army and a Switzerland that uses the resources it spends on the military for the promotion of peace instead. Switzerland is rich enough to buy fighter aircraft, but it would be far better to use these resources to deal with the dangers arising out of the huge gap between North and South and the risks of ecological destruction. The need to invest our resources in solving these problems is so great that we cannot afford to waste money on the latest weapons technology for our defence in western Europe – particularly since the threats these weapons are supposed to deter no longer exist. I am convinced that a war between Austria, Italy and Switzerland or between France and Germany is as unlikely as a war between the citizens of Zurich and Basle. Once we recognise that we do not need an army because the threats of the past no longer exist, the sooner we will free resources for preventive measures against future conflicts developing in those areas where the risk of conflict is still real – for example in the former Soviet Union. The situation in Bosnia, which is probably what cost us victory in the F/A-18 vote, is an indication of what could happen in the former Soviet Union and is something Switzerland can help to prevent.

Switzerland does not need an army to deal with waves of refugees threatening to flood the country from the East. A civil defence corps would be sufficient. I am not against a civil defence corps as such, I am just against the current focus of the civil defence corps on survival after an atomic attack. Such a corps could be used to deal with refugees or to provide assistance after natural catastrophes. But we must not forget that the refugees are messengers of injustice and that we should do everything possible to prevent the injustice in the first place, then we would not have the refugee problem. Investing resources in that makes more sense than buying new weapons systems.

Switzerland clearly has to change its understanding of neutrality in foreign policy. Swiss neutrality is a product of the nineteenth century, based on the idea that while two are fighting the Swiss stay on the sidelines. But this concept has become completely absurd in the twentieth century and will be more so in the next century. We have to understand that neutrality now means solidarity.

The idea that seems to be under consideration in the Swiss government now is to establish a closer relationship with NATO and for Switzerland to participate in European security policy. This would be a leap from one extreme to the other. It would be the leap from extreme neutrality into membership of the only existing offensive military alliance in the world. NATO is clearly an offensive and not a defensive military alliance.

The most important duty for the Swiss over the next few years is to join the United Nations[9] and a more democratic European Union, not NATO. The UN is the future for the world community, but it needs to rejuvenate itself and find a new way of dealing effectively with international relations over the next ten years. The current crisis of the UN is not a crisis of democracy or of the core ideals of the UN, but a crisis of having too much to do and insufficient resources to meet the task. And in this area Switzerland, with its tradition of international conflict mediation, has something to offer.

Notes

1. In the mid-1970s some 12 per cent of Swiss men were declared unfit for military service.

2. Conscientious objectors face a military tribunal and are usually sent-

enced to some six months' imprisonment and must pay a fee representing compensation to the state for not fulfilling their duty of military service. Since 1991, however, the military tribunals which sentence conscientious objectors have commuted most gaol terms into obligatory community service. A civilian service alternative to military or civil defence is currently before parliament. Once passed it is expected to require applicants to spend one and a half times the usual military service period engaged in community service. Those unfit to carry out their military service for health reasons can serve in the civil defence corps instead. Swiss men who are fit for military service now spend a minimum of around 300 days in the army between the ages of 20 and 42. The basic training lasts 15 weeks and subsequently there are 10 refresher courses of 19 days each. Officers must serve for longer periods. After completing military service Swiss men must spend another 10 years in civil defence units. The army has cut the duration of military service. Previously a Swiss man could expect to be performing military service in the army until he was 50 and then civil defence until he was 60.

3. *Halbgefangenschaft* requires the convicted to spend nights and weekends in prison but allows them out on weekdays to go to work.

4. During the First World War many leading German Swiss favoured Germany, while the French Swiss supported France. The sympathies of leading military officers, who had been greatly influenced by the Prussian military on which the Swiss army had been modelled, clearly lay with the German Kaiser. The head of the military department of Canton Berne wrote in his diary in August 1914: 'On general cultural grounds as well as political I believe that a German victory is desirable.' During the First World War the Swiss military provided the German army with secret military intelligence in accordance with a secret agreement of 1910 (see Steinberg, 1976, p. 39).

5. At the Congress of Vienna in 1815, called to redraw the map of Europe after the defeat of Napoleon, the European powers approved a Swiss request for the country's neutrality to be officially recognised. The roots of the neutrality stretch back at least as far as the Thirty Years' War of 1618–48 when the confederation's policy of neutrality and its value as a source of mercenaries ensured it was not invaded by any of the parties to the conflict.

6. On 24 November 1969 the Federal Council decided to sign the 1968 Nuclear Non-Proliferation Treaty.

7. The General Strike of November 1918 was organised partly in imitation of the 1917 Bolshevik Revolution in Russia and was influenced by contacts between Vladimir Lenin, who lived in Switzerland from 1914 to 1917, and leading Swiss Social Democrats. The three-day strike brought some 250,000 workers on to the streets. They faced around 100,000 troops. However, an ultimatum by the Federal Council broke the back of the strike which was then unconditionally abandoned. Some of the strikers' demands – proportional representation in parliament and a 48-hour week – were, however, later passed by parliament. In Geneva in November 1932, at a time when the global

economic crisis had driven Swiss unemployment to record heights, troops fired on a demonstration of unemployed workers, killing ten and wounding over a hundred.

8. In a bitter 1989 referendum, on a proposal by the GSoA to abolish the Swiss army, an unexpectedly large 35.6 per cent voted in favour of the suggestion. The GSoA also collected the necessary signatures to force a referendum in 1993 on government plans to buy 34 McDonnell Douglas F/A-18 Hornet jet fighters for around 3.5 billion Swiss francs. GSoA's proposal, that was put to referendum, was for a moratorium on all purchases of military aircraft until the year 2000. The proposal was defeated but some 42 per cent voted in favour.

9. The Swiss electorate overwhelmingly rejected membership of the United Nations in a referendum in 1986. The Swiss government in its 1993 foreign policy report set UN membership as a long-term foreign policy goal.

THE GENERAL

Arthur Liener

Chief of staff General Arthur Liener, 58 years old, is one of the country's highest-ranking military officers. He is also a trained physicist who did not start a full-time career in the army until he was 33 years old. 'I am a physicist and still feel myself to be an academic. I, too, am surprised at my career. I did not look for it. I was a militia officer and when I was asked to take on the full-time job I simply made myself available, partly reluctantly, partly with a certain enthusiasm.' Liener, a large, corpulent man with unruly white hair, speaks in his large third-floor office at the military department in Berne. He leans back in his leather armchair and speaks with a loud, commanding voice. A stubby cigar is either wedged between the fingers of his right hand while he is talking or firmly clamped between his lips when he is not. Occasionally he leans forward and reaches for matches on the table in front of him.

Switzerland does not have a large army. That is a common and widespread misconception. At the moment we have an army of 600,000 troops,[1] although that is being reduced. But if you want to compare that with, for example, Germany's *Bundeswehr* then you have to make a comparison with their mobilisation strength which is considerably over one million troops. If you take the 380,000 that the *Bundeswehr* has today as a standing military force then the comparable force for us lies at around 25,000 men. That is the soldiers doing basic training in the recruit schools plus those doing refresher courses. So we have a standing army of 25,000 to 30,000 men. One has to be careful that one does not compare apples with oranges.

Per capita of the country's population the Swiss army is perhaps large but that is because Switzerland has a militia army. It is this militia system, rather than the size, that is the key to Swiss society. All Swiss men have to do military service. They start basic training in the recruits' school when they are 20 years old and they finish their military service in the army when they are 42 years old. The militia system divides military service duties equally and imposes the obligation on every male Swiss citizen to contribute to the country's security. This is at the core of Swiss democracy and is undoubtedly a major factor behind the political stability of Switzerland as a country. The most fascinating thing about this army is that it allows managers and workers to meet on a level playing field. And this is an inspiration for me and for my work every day.

Let me give you an example. When I was on a general staff course there were two drivers. One was then the general manager of IBM in Switzerland, the other drove a beer delivery truck; both shared the same quarters during their military service. Later I met the IBM director and asked him about that time. He said: 'That was one of the most interesting experiences of my life.' He said the beer lorry driver had felt the same way. Their experience was typical. If you look at any normal unit today on a refresher course you will find a mixture of backgrounds, languages, education and jobs – it is fascinating, stimulating and very healthy for the people involved. I think that this aspect of the Swiss army is unique in the world and that it is worth preserving.

I certainly have no intention of presiding over the transformation of our militia army into a professional army, as some people seem to want. I don't believe you can delegate the security of the state – the preservation of its sovereignty – to others, for example to a professional army rather than a militia army. Incidentally, the military department has analysed the cost of setting up a professional army and we found that with the current defence budget we would only be able to finance a small professional army of about 50,000 soldiers.

Of course, one should not forget that Switzerland has a long military tradition and there are many Swiss who like to feel they are part of that tradition. In the Middle Ages Switzerland's only export was mercenaries. In central Switzerland there were a number of famous families who earned their money by selling the services of Swiss soldiers to fight the battles of various European royal courts.

And at a time when Switzerland was not at all wealthy, for many young Swiss men serving as a mercenary was the only way to earn a living. Swiss troops won a reputation as tough, fearless fighters on European battlefields. But that reputation suffered a major setback when the Swiss were beaten by the French who used a revolutionary combination of artillery and cavalry at the battle of Marignano[2] in north Italy in 1515. But the defeat did not stop the mercenary tradition which continued into the eighteenth century.[3]

The history of the current Swiss army dates from the time after the 1798 defeat by Napoleon when, in principle, the old Swiss confederation died. I think one could say the current Swiss federal army was created in the wake of the 1815 Congress of Vienna when Europe's and Switzerland's borders were redrawn. But the army did not really see battle until the *Sonderbundskrieg* in the middle of the eighteenth century. Under Dufour the Swiss cross, which we have as our national flag, was used as the official symbol for federal troops for the first time.[4]

Towards the end of the nineteenth century the army was undoubtedly influenced by the military success of the Prussian army in the 1860s and 1870s. Success always attracts attention and imitators, and it is undoubtedly true that the officers and generals of the Swiss army were more influenced by Prussian military thinking than by military developments in other European countries. I am sure that certain things were copied from the Prussian army. But the Swiss army has always been open to foreign influences. Our present officers' cap is taken from the French military and the uniforms our soldiers have been wearing since the Second World War are clearly modelled on those of the American GI.

The idea of abolishing the Swiss army is, of course, nonsense. We are not faced with a direct military threat at the moment, but can you give me a guarantee that we will not be in the future? I have something against those people – such as the *Gruppe fuer eine Schweiz ohne Armee* – who are always so convinced they know best how we should run our affairs. The same people in early 1989 sent a message of greeting to comrade Erich Honecker in East Berlin. There is a member of the lower house of parliament who in the spring of 1989 sent a hymn of praise to Honecker and in November the Berlin Wall fell. And these people want to tell us that they can see clearly how the future will develop and that they know what is best for the army.

I see attacks against the existence of the army and attacks against the role it plays in maintaining a democratic consensus in Swiss society as an attempt ultimately to destroy this system and to introduce class conflict into Swiss society. I feel sorry for these critics that they don't take the opportunity to work in a military unit and see how people from the most varied of social, economic and political backgrounds have to pitch in together and carry out a task. They often swear at each other, at times they probably hate each other, but somehow they have to find a way of working together.

And – let me say it again – it is precisely this that is the great strength of the militia system and that is why I am not prepared to put the question of the future of the militia system on the table for discussion. The advantages of this system for Switzerland, added to the need for very rapid mobilisation because of the relatively small size of this country, greatly outweigh any disadvantages of a militia system. The longer I work within this system and learn about it, the more I am convinced it is right for Switzerland. I firmly believe that the militia system has contributed to the lack of serious social conflicts in Switzerland over the last 150 years. People throughout society know and respect each other. I am very proud of this aspect of the Swiss army.

One should also not forget that the Swiss army probably ensured that Switzerland was not invaded by Nazi Germany during the Second World War. The defensive strategy, or the combat position, at that time was known as the *reduit* (redoubt). In 1940 when the country was completely surrounded by the Axis powers the Swiss supreme military commander, a General Henri Guisans, asked himself the question: 'What can I do with the limited military forces at my disposal to maintain at least part of Switzerland sovereign and independent?' His answer was to withdraw most of the Swiss army from the frontier and have it dig into defences built in solid rock in the Alps in central Switzerland. I am sure that the Axis forces would have had a very hard time taking Switzerland without suffering exceptionally high losses and casualties. So at the very least the Swiss army forced Axis forces to make a detour around Switzerland – and at the most they dissuaded the Nazis from invading.[5]

Of course it is true that the nature of the potential strategic threat facing Switzerland has now changed. The *reduit* is no longer

relevant today. It was given up in the second half of 1944 and the
army was posted along the whole length of the Swiss border again
as the Axis powers withdrew. And since then there has been no
more *reduit* thinking. In fact if you look at the strategic thinking
now you can see that it aims at protecting every centimetre of this
country's territory. Even under the reformed army of *Armee 95*
that is still the goal. We will no longer be able to provide total
area defence because we will no longer have enough resources as a
result of the reforms. But we still intend to defend every centimetre
of the country's territory and to place particular emphasis on
certain important areas – this is the so-called dynamic area defence.
For that we need a high degree of mobility so that we can get
forces to the borders as quickly as possible and to specific important areas.

This is the classical strategic picture. But it is clear that with
the collapse of the Warsaw Pact and the fall of the Iron Curtain a
completely new strategic situation has been created. For Switzerland the new post-Cold War dangers are risks below the level of
war. No one can say exactly what these will be, but I think it is
utopian to claim that certain worst-case scenarios are neither possible nor conceivable. The world has become considerably more
complex and the dangers considerably greater. Previously the world
was really rather tolerable – it was calculable. We had a bipolar
system and as long as that remained relatively in balance, which it
was more or less, things were fine. You just had to ensure that the
forces were more or less equal. But now this equilibrium has been
replaced by an imbalance, and we face a whole series of potential
problems which could explode in very unpredictable and volatile
ways very quickly. I am not really thinking of waves of refugees
from the East. The refugee problem is certainly one that worries
me, but it is a problem that we can handle. I see other dangers. I
see for example the danger of ethnic conflicts abroad spilling over
into our country. In other words I fear that ethnic groups will
suddenly start fighting out their battles in Switzerland and not just
in their own countries. This is not just a danger for Switzerland. It
could also affect France, Germany or any number of other
countries.

We have had a perfect example of what I mean with the recent
Turkish embassy shooting here in Berne.[6] The fact that the Kurds
were able to organise simultaneous demonstrations and protests

throughout western Europe is a clear enough indication of the kind of potential danger we are facing.

It is true that we probably do not need F/A-18s to control the kinds of dangers I have just mentioned. But the F/A-18 debate was about completely different issues. It was really about Swiss neutrality. As long as Switzerland wants to pursue an independent policy, a neutral policy, we must be in the position of having the necessary means to enforce this policy. I think it is not credible to believe in Swiss neutrality if Switzerland does not exist in the third dimension, that is if Swiss sovereignty ends fifty or a hundred metres above ground level. If you say 'no' to modernising our air force we would have to rely on our national sport *Hornussen* for air defence, as that is about the height one can throw a *Schindel*.[7] But then the army can no longer be expected to ensure that a government decision to deny overflight rights to NATO or other countries is respected. We did not, for example, allow overflight rights during the Gulf War and in the Bosnian conflict we have also not granted certain overflight rights. This meant that Switzerland had to be flown around. If we have no credible air force we can forbid other countries from flying in our airspace as much as we want, but it will be like trying to chew a piece of hard bread without teeth.

At the moment Switzerland still has a policy of neutrality and I think Switzerland will find it very difficult to loosen the bonds of neutrality. I don't think it necessarily should. Anyway it is also good for Europe, I think, if there is a state which wants to maintain its autonomy and independence. This does not mean that neutrality is identical with isolationism, rather it is a matter of pursuing a policy of neutrality that is appropriate to the current degree of integration of Switzerland into western Europe. In the long term Switzerland may decide that it can best ensure its security through closer cooperation with Europe. Some kind of security policy cooperation is certainly possible and closer ties with NATO would clearly be one option.

But the collapse of the Warsaw Pact has stimulated is new thinking on weapons for the Swiss army. One can't equip the army unless one has concrete ideas of what threats could materialise. The army is currently equipped on the assumption that it would have to face the forces of the Warsaw Pact. Therefore we still have a very strong anti-tank defence system and a relatively large infantry. We are now in the process of adapting the army's weapons, but this takes time, particularly with a militia army. However, if I look around at the armies of Austria, Germany, Italy and France, they are also all still armed to face a Warsaw Pact invasion.

As far as the case of Jeanmaire is concerned I think the issue is very clear. There is no excuse for his behaviour. I don't want to comment on whether the information he gave to the Russian was significant or not; the thing I do condemn is that a man of his rank could do something like that. After all during the War people were shot for treason and so one cannot then react softly and give an officer special treatment, rather one should be tough – in fact even tougher than normal. It is proven that Jeanmaire handed over classified documents and I think it is right that he should have been given a harsher sentence than someone of a lower rank. I can't really judge whether the sentence he received was too harsh or not as I have no access to the evidence. However, there is probably room for discussion over whether the sentence was too severe. But it is not a question of the sentence, it is a question of the act – and the act was wrong.

Notes

1. The military department has implemented a programme of reforms aimed at cutting costs and modernising the army. The programme, *Armee 95*, has reduced the size of the army's mobilisation force from 600,000 to around 450,000 by lowering the age until which Swiss men must perform military service from 52 to 42. In the 1970s the army's mobilisation strength was 650,000.

2. After a series of victories in northern Italy Swiss forces, fighting for the ruler of Milan, Massimiliano Sforza, were defeated at the battle of Marignano in 1515 by the army of King François I of France who employed a combination, revolutionary for the time, of infantry, artillery and cavalry.

3. According to some estimates over two million Swiss soldiers, 70,000 officers and 700 generals fought as mercenaries between the fifteenth and the eighteenth centuries (see Flueeler and Gfeller-Corhesy, 1975, p. 344). In 1859 Switzerland made it illegal for its citizens to serve in foreign armies. Despite this many Swiss fought in the Spanish Civil War in the late 1930s, although this time not as mercenaries. At the start of the Civil War the Federal Council explicitly forbade Swiss from participating in the conflict, fearing Swiss neutrality would be compromised and the resources for Switzerland's own defence would be undermined. Some 400 Swiss were found guilty of breaking this law between 1936 and 1939. The issue has remained a bitter one to the

present day, but a number of attempts to win an amnesty for those found guilty have so far failed.

4. General Guillaume Henri Dufour commanded the Protestant forces in the 1847 Swiss civil war, the *Sonderbundskrieg*. (For details on the *Sonderbundskrieg*, see note 1 to The Vicar in chapter 3.) The Swiss flag, a white cross on a red background, was established as the official flag of the Swiss confederation in 1848. It has been traced back to the fourteenth century when some soldiers are believed to have sewn a cross on to their tunics to help them to recognise each other in battle. The cross is said to be in memory of the Roman Thebian legion and its leader, Mauritius, the patron saint of the infantry. The legion, which had converted to Christianity, was massacred by non-Christian units faithful to the Roman Empire in what is now Canton Valais in southwest Switzerland. The red background of the Swiss flag is one of the three colours of the Holy Roman Empire and symbolises independence and justice (see Maeder and Mattern, 1993, pp. 54–63).

5. Historical research after the Second World War discovered that the Wehrmacht considered occupying Switzerland in the summer of 1940. An invasion plan, code named Operation Tannenbaum, had already been prepared. Franz Halder, the chief of the German general staff, said after the War: 'I was constantly hearing of outbursts of Hitler's fury against Switzerland, which, given his mentality, might have led at any minute to military activities for the army' (see Steinberg, 1976, p. 49).

6. On 24 June 1993 Semsettin Kurt, a 29-year-old Kurd, was killed by shots fired from the Turkish embassy compound in Berne during an anti-Turkish demonstration by Kurds outside the embassy. The protest was part of an apparently coordinated set of attacks and demonstrations against Turkish offices by Kurds in a number of western European cities.

7. *Hornussen*, a Swiss national sport, is played with a puck and a steel or graphite whip. The puck is hit downfield with the whip. Opponents in the field try to block the flight of the puck, which can reach speeds of up to 200 kph, with *Schindel*, spade-like boards. The name *Hornussen* comes from *Hornisse* (hornet), and is attributable to the hornet-like sound the pebbles, that were originally used as pucks, made when in flight. Today the pucks are made of synthetic materials. The sport is believed to have developed from an old war game in which soldiers practised defending themselves against flying objects fired at them by the enemy.

Chapter 7

'THE OTHER MAGIC MOUNTAIN'

Tuberculosis was the scourge of Europe in the late nineteenth and the first half of the twentieth century. At its height the disease killed every seventh European. Medical science was helpless.

Almost by chance a German doctor, Dr Alexander Spengler, who had fled to Switzerland following the collapse of the 1848 revolution in Germany, noticed that the inhabitants of a small Alpine village where he had found work as a country doctor appeared strangely almost untouched by the plague. At first he wondered whether ammonia vapours helped and so encouraged people to stand in cow sheds to inhale the ammonia fumes of cow dung. But soon Spengler was convinced the secret lay in the sunshine and fresh air of Davos. He brought his first two patients to the town in 1865 and developed a regime of rest combined with good food. In 1882 he founded the Alexanderhausklinik, the first tuberculosis clinic in Davos.

Spengler's treatment, however, had one drawback: it failed to address the problem of contagion. Those suffering from tuberculosis were soon flocking to Davos and staying in hotels alongside healthy tourists. It was not until the arrival of another doctor, Dr Karl Turban, that hotels began to be converted into sanatoriums and patients were kept in virtual quarantine to reduce the risk of infection. Turban began the close monitoring of patients' temperatures for indications on the course of the illness. By the turn of the century the closed sanatoriums were the model for treatment of tuberculosis until after the Second World War when the introduction of new antibiotics offered a more effective way of treating the illness.

Tuberculosis, also known as 'The Sombre Majesty' or the 'White Plague',[1] made Davos cosmopolitan. Sir Arthur Conan Doyle, Robert Louis Stevenson (who wrote *Treasure Island* while in the town), Franz Kafka, Thomas Mann, Fyodor Dostoyevsky, Anton Chekhov, Maxim Gorky and Vladimir Lenin (who came to visit a close colleague called Mischa Sawodski) all spent time in Davos. Patients came mainly from Germany, but also from as far away as Shanghai and Buenos Aires.

The publication of Thomas Mann's novel *Der Zauberberg* (*The Magic Mountain*) in 1924 transformed Davos into a cult, particularly in the German-speaking world. The book was not popular in Davos, however. The authorities feared it painted Davos as a town of illness and death; doctors and sanatoriums felt they had been criticised for not caring more for the psychological well-being of their patients. Some doctors, who considered demanding a retraction from Mann or taking legal steps, banned the book from their sanatoriums and forbade patients to read it.

Helga Ferdmann, an authority on the sanatorium era in Davos, arrived in the town from Germany in 1931 and spent the rest of her life in Davos working as a nurse on occasions and as a journalist. In this chapter she remembers a period in the town's history which disappeared following the introduction of chemotherapy treatment for tuberculosis after the Second World War – a period which saw thousands of Swiss and foreigners fighting for their lives in the town.

Note

1. See Ferdmann (1989), p. 9.

SWITZERLAND AND TUBERCULOSIS

Helga Ferdmann

Helga Ferdmann, 84 years old, speaks in her second-floor flat in an old building in the centre of Davos. She leaves her visitors to hang their coats at the steamed glass front door and makes her way slowly to the lounge. 'My knees', she says in explanation as she sinks into one of the chairs around a table. In one corner of the heavily furnished room next to a window there is a small table covered with papers and an old typewriter where she works. Her face is very wrinkled. She is hard of hearing and frequently cocks her ear whenever she fails to catch a question. But her recollections, which she delivers while twisting a ring on her finger, are very articulate. She speaks frequently of her husband who died over thirty years ago, but never mentions his name.

I have known nothing else but tuberculosis almost since the beginning of my life. My whole family died of tuberculosis. I was born in Saarbruecken in Germany, a region that had one of the highest rates of tuberculosis in Europe between the wars. It was something to do with the bad air and all the industry there. My family – my mother, my father, everyone – died of tuberculosis. My mother used to get up in the morning and spend two whole hours, from 6 until 8 o'clock, just coughing and trying to catch her breath. She was divorced and had to support the family alone and she was terribly ill. It was awful to see how she suffered. It was probably the hard life she led more than the tuberculosis that killed her.

After my mother died in 1928 I moved to Essen to live with relatives there. But I had very little money and not much to eat; I was starving really. I would have loved to have studied medicine, but after the death of my mother there was no money and it simply was not possible. A cousin of mine was running a small hotel here in Davos, and she wrote and asked me to come and help her for a year. She said it would be a good idea for me to come to Davos, because if I had any tuberculosis in my lungs I would be sure to get rid of it. So I came to Davos in 1931 when I was 21 years old and, after the experience of my mother's illness, I was glad to go somewhere where I felt safe from the disease.

In my cousin's small hotel I met my future husband. He was Russian and had come to Davos in 1915 to get treatment for his tuberculosis. His father had paid for him to come to Switzerland. After the Bolshevik Revolution he stayed on in Davos, but it was not so much the Revolution as his tuberculosis that kept him here. In 1925 he founded a local magazine called the *Davoser Revue*, which still exists today. I am very proud that it is still going because it is something he created.

He was twenty years older than me and in some senses that was good and in others the reverse. But every marriage has difficulties you have to deal with. For me it was no problem, however, that he was ill. I had experienced so much tuberculosis at home with my family that his illness was nothing new. I was also not afraid of infection. But my husband suffered. He only had one functioning lung and that had tuberculosis as well. He had a terribly difficult time with his breathing and climbing steps was a real struggle. Every day was a battle for him. But he was a hero. Although he was so ill, he ignored the illness and acted as if it did not exist. There were many silent heroes in Davos – people who lived with their disease, fought it with quiet dignity and ignored the fact that they were often very close to death.

For us both it was also a financial battle. It was very hard to make ends meet with the *Davoser Revue* and we did not have much money. A magazine is probably one of the least profitable businesses you can run. From the first day of our marriage I was in the office of the magazine and then after work I had to do the household chores as well. But if I had not worked we would have starved.

Like many of the Russians here, who after the 1917 Revolution were cut off from their financial support, my husband gave chess lessons to help make ends meet. He was in the local chess club and gave lessons to patients staying in the Hotel Schatzalp, which was built around the turn of the century and is one of the few hotels here which has retained some of the atmosphere and style of the sanatorium period. My husband earned about five francs a day from chess lessons. After the Bolshevik Revolution the Red Cross provided a little assistance to some Russians, but most found it difficult and had to move into ever cheaper accommodation. For their chess lessons they would wander from terrace to terrace and give lessons to the patients who were lying there for their sunshine cure.

I have no children. My husband had one daughter from his previous marriage and he said it would make no sense to have more children while we were earning so little. And so I brought up the daughter by his first wife. She, my husband's first wife, had died in childbirth because the doctors made a mistake when she went into labour. The daughter was small, only a few years old when we married. I regretted not having children of my own – in fact I suffered because of not having children. 'Suffer' is perhaps a strong term, but it was painful for me to look into a baby carriage. It's normal. You can say what you like, a normal woman wants children and not having children was very painful for me. But I understood my husband's view. I had to work a lot to earn enough money for us to survive and it would not have been possible for me to raise a crowd of children as well.

The *Davoser Revue*, which was a magazine for fellow tuberculosis sufferers, published poems, essays and all kinds of thoughts written by the patients in Davos. It was my husband's reaction to Thomas Mann's novel *Der Zauberberg*.

When *Der Zauberberg* was published in 1924 it was not very popular here. Many felt Thomas Mann had only showed the life of the wealthy patients in Davos. He came to Davos in 1912, while he was writing *Death in Venice*, to visit his wife Katja who was here to cure a suspected lung tuberculosis. Interestingly, as far as the tuberculosis of Katja is concerned, the X-rays of her chest, which resurfaced some years ago and were analysed by a doctor, showed that she had no tuberculosis in her lungs. So you could say that *Der Zauberberg* was the product of a misdiagnosis.

The authorities here did not like Thomas Mann's novel because they felt it gave Davos a reputation for illness, represented it as a town where there was a grave risk of infection. I remember the mother of a friend of mine who came to Davos in the late 1940s for treatment saying to her son before he left for Davos: 'Be careful when you get there. In Davos people spit a lot and that is very dangerous.' And someone once told me, quite seriously, that the patients in the sanatoria used soup plates as spittoons and that if one was working there one had to be very careful not to get infected from that. It was all nonsense, of course.

Many people also felt Thomas Mann was unfair with his view of the so-called *Zauberberg* illness – the idea that people here were made to feel ill and did not try to recover. There were other people here, who were perhaps less wealthy, and who had no choice but to show great self-discipline if they were to survive at all, despite their illness. As Somerset Maugham once said, it is easier to cry if you have money, regardless of how things stand.[1]

I remember one family I knew from Saarbruecken in Germany where five daughters had all come down with tuberculosis, one after the other. One after the other they also died. I remember seeing the mother in despair after the fourth died. At the funeral she lifted the body out of the coffin and clasped it in her arms and cried for God to explain why she must die. I met the fifth daughter again, later, here in Davos and saw how she struggled to survive. She was always gasping for air, going through terrible operations, and during the War she ran out of money because her brothers could no longer send her any. But she always found ways of surviving. When I stood at her death bed I remember thinking she looked like an angel.

There were so many patients here who despite their illness simply had to find ways of surviving. They lived in modest rooms and heated small ovens with acorns they had collected themselves from the woods. They ate bread and milk mostly and earned a bit of money working in the households of wealthy families where occasionally they would also be given a proper meal. For them, of course, the cure took much longer and was much harder. I know of some former patients who felt bitter and who refused to see the film of Thomas Mann's novel because it showed nothing of their Davos, the Davos in which they could not afford even a single visit to a coffee shop and were happy if they had enough money for stamps and toothpaste.[2]

When I wrote *Der andere Zauberberg* (*The Other Magic Mountain*) in 1989 I was trying to show that Thomas Mann's picture of the sanatorium period of Davos was one-sided. Not only did he ignore the poor patients and only show the society of the wealthy patients, he also did not pay any attention to the local people. Again and again I asked local people, intellectuals, and people whom you would have expected to have had contact with someone like Thomas Mann, but I never found anyone who had had any contact with Thomas Mann when he was here in 1912. There was a division between the foreign patients who came to Davos for treatment and the local people living here. And one group had little contact with the other.

Generally the local people in Davos were very hospitable to the tuberculosis patients. There were stories of local people not wanting to sit in the same churches as patients. It was true that open tuberculosis, an advanced stage of the disease, was contagious. The doctors told the patients not to touch or go near babies because of the danger of infection. A sneeze or some phlegm, for example, would have been enough to infect not only babies but also the doctors. And you could often see people in the streets with white gauze pads over their noses and mouths, presumably to protect themselves from the sick. There were also many from the lowlands who were so ignorant and afraid of the disease that they thought they would catch it the moment they arrived in Davos. But the local people were earning a lot of money from the sanatorium business and this alone ensured that they were hospitable and friendly.

But Thomas Mann was right about the active love-life of patients. Some people said tuberculosis stimulated relationships among patients, particularly in the more expensive sanatoriums. The fear of death that was hanging over everyone also made many people say to themselves that this was their last chance to enjoy life before they died. Another reason was, of course, that the cure often took years and the long separations from family and home made many people more promiscuous. People who had a real tuberculosis had to stay in Davos for long periods. It took a long time for the sunshine and fresh air, that was the major part of the cure, to take effect and heal the disease.

Many of the tuberculosis patients never left at all. They came to Davos for treatment and then stayed on. Every second house here has someone who was not originally from Davos but who was cured by the sun and air here and then decided to stay. Partly it was fear that the tuberculosis would break out again once they left Davos and returned to the lowlands, and partly it was because

Davos was and is a wonderful place to live and has a special atmosphere. I am happy here in Davos and I never want to leave. It is like that for all of us. Davos is a unique combination of village and town: everyone knows one another, and on the street one bumps into people one knows and one is not as anonymous as in the city.

The famous Davos cure, the sunshine and fresh air cure, was discovered by Dr Alexander Spengler[3] and then developed by him and other doctors. It was the main form of treatment for tuberculosis until chemotherapy appeared soon after the Second World War.

The daily regime of the cure was very strict. At 6.45 a.m. the sister came and your temperature and pulse rate were taken and both were recorded in your medical records. Then you got up for breakfast and immediately after breakfast went out on to the balcony or terrace of your sanatorium and sat or lay on the famous Davos *chaise-longue* absorbing the sun's rays and the fresh air. New patients who had just arrived from the lowlands usually had to stay in their rooms at first because the fresh air was very aggressive and could trigger a haemorrhage. These patients had to adjust to the altitude of Davos and to the air, and then gradually they would be allowed out. So you lay in the fresh air and sunshine until around 10 o'clock and then you were allowed about one hour of free time when you could leave the sanatorium. New patients would be more strictly controlled in this respect too and only allowed out for ten or twenty minutes at first, and then week by week they would gradually be given more and more free time to the maximum of one hour.

The treatment continued with lunch and then a silent rest cure on the terrace until around 3 o'clock. The silence was very strictly adhered to. It was the time when the weakest and most seriously ill were allowed out and you had to be quiet for them. Some read books, others wrote or occupied themselves with little handicrafts. Another hour or so of free time followed. By 5 o'clock everyone had to be back in the sanatorium. Dinner was at around 7 in the evening and then often there was another period on the *chaise-longue* until 9 o'clock, but this time indoors.

Many patients became obsessed with the thermometer which was used to measure their progress and to see whether they were recovering or not. The seriously ill had temperatures of 37.1 to

37.5; below that you were doing well. My husband never studied his temperature or did a rest cure. He simply acted as if he was not ill, although he was in fact very ill. But many did.

For some it was crucial, however, because they knew that if they did not get better – if their open tuberculosis[4] remained open – the doctors would recommend surgery. Much of this surgery was brutal. A friend of mine had his ribs on one side removed to collapse the diseased lung and stop it moving, to restrain the spread of the disease. This was the so-called *Rippen Resektion* (surgical removal of the ribs), which many tuberculosis patients went through. It often left them with a crooked walk. Many other patients were given the 'tyre' treatment, something my husband also had. Air was pumped into the patient's body wall around the chest to create a kind of 'tyre of air' and in this way the lungs were kept quiet.[5] This could be very uncomfortable, even dangerous for the patient. I remember one Christmas, soon after I had arrived in Davos and was still living in my cousin's hotel, we had arranged for a Father Christmas to come, but he arrived early and said he would not be able to play the part because he had just been pumped up with air and was finding it very difficult to breathe. The patient was usually filled with air once a week; if too much was pumped in then the patient experienced a terrible crushing sensation and could hardly breathe until some of the air had been absorbed by the body.

The main element of the cure, however, was rest, sunshine and fresh air coupled with good food. Hours were spent on the *chaise-longues*. Sanatoria competed with each other with guarantees of more sunshine hours per day than other hotels and sanatoriums. And Davos could compete well with other sanatorium centres because of its unique geography. It is in the only valley in Switzerland which runs from north to south and which opens up towards the south, allowing the sun's rays unhindered access for the whole day. This is the secret of Davos's climate. It was enough simply to be in Davos and to breathe the air here and eat healthily. The amount of food eaten by some of the patients in the sanatoriums, however, was really excessive – they ate such huge amounts of food it was almost disgusting.

Tuberculosis is a disease that really only attacks weakened bodies, or bodies where the immune system is weak. Today tuberculosis is still treated here, with Davos particularly attracting old men who are suffering from the disease or chronic bronchitis. The people who catch tuberculosis these days are really only people who are undernourished or drunkards as it is an illness that attacks people who are physically weak.

Strangely it is also a place that many Jews come to. For a long time I did not know why so many Jewish families came here. Then one summer day I saw a Jewish family on the street and I stopped them and asked them why so many Jews are attracted to Davos. The father said: 'It is like this. So many of us have been killed that we have to ensure our children grow up to be healthy. And the healthiest place for them is Davos.' Children seem to react particularly positively to the air and sunshine here and Davos is the only place in Switzerland today that has a children's sanatorium. You can really experience miracles with the treatment of children here today.

But death was always near. I never really knew how much longer my husband would live. He died in 1962 when he was 73 years old. He never felt he wanted to return to Russia. He remained in contact with his father and with his sister – she wrote a lot – but he never saw them again. We had a different attitude to death because it was always present; we never knew who would be taken next. Of those that came here for treatment, many were cured but many were not: the outcome depended on the seriousness of the tuberculosis and on the attitude the patient had to his or her illness. Quite a lot could be achieved with a positive attitude – you had to believe that you would be cured here. Many were cured but many died as well, as you can see if you visit the Davos cemetery which is very large for a relatively small town.

You were closer to death here than in the lowlands. Occasionally you saw patients suffer a violent haemorrhage when a blood vessel burst and they coughed up masses of blood. Usually these were patients who had not kept to the strict rules of the cure or who had drunk alcohol. The rules of the treatment were very strict and if you broke them you could be expelled from the sanatorium. I remember my husband telling me of a number of cases where patients had been forced to find another place to stay in Davos – or even in another village nearby – because they had overstepped the regulations of a sanatorium and been expelled by the head doctor.

Illness was a part of the everyday street scene. You could see who was tubercular from their distinctive hollow cheeks. You could hear their rasping coughs and see the fever in their eyes. But, of course, their appearance and symptoms also depended on the kind of tuberculosis they were suffering from. For a while I worked as a nurse in a sanatorium where I saw many different kinds of tuberculosis. A genital tuberculosis is very different from a lung tuberculosis or a tuberculosis of the larynx.

Ironically, while so many people here worried about their disease and whether they were recovering or not, a doctor once told me that everyone in Davos had had a tuberculosis. The disease did not break out in all cases but often remained dormant. I long thought that I was the only person in my family not to have caught tuberculosis, but it was not true. I had also had a tuberculosis – it had simply never broken out.

The hotels in Davos today want to forget the history of tuberculosis and sanatoria and want Davos to be known as a ski and mountaineering resort. They often get quite angry with me when I write or talk publicly about the sanatorium past of Davos. I don't take any notice of them, of course. You can't deny your past, it exists and you have to face up to it. Most of the hotels here were previously sanatoria and have now been remodelled as sports hotels. After the War and the introduction of chemotherapy treatment for tuberculosis, one after another the sanatoria began converting themselves into hotels for tourists. Many people were still coming to Davos after the War and as late as the 1950s to receive treatment for their tuberculosis although the treatment with streptomycin[6] and penicillin had been discovered by the end of the War. The chemotherapy did not lead to an immediate collapse of the sanatorium period in Davos, although it was, of course, the beginning of the end. Patients with tuberculosis in the lowlands were no longer sent up to Davos for the cure but were treated with antibiotics in the hospitals there. There were some patients who for a while had both treatments – chemotherapy and sunshine and fresh air here in Davos – but the numbers dropped rapidly.[7]

Few people living here in Davos now are aware of the history of this town and that Davos was a place that saved the lives of many people. I always remember my husband's words: 'There is no place on earth where sick people have performed so much good and healthy work than here in Davos.'

Notes

1. From Ferdmann (1989), p. 9.

2. Some of the poorer patients lived in one of the people's sanatoria (*Volks-sanatorium*), of which there were a few. The first one, the Basle Sanatorium, was opened in 1896.

3. Dr Alexander Spengler, a German, originally came to Switzerland and Davos as a refugee following the collapse of the 1848 revolution in Germany. As a country doctor in Davos he was surprised to see that tuberculosis, the plague of Europe at the time, appeared to have left most of the population untouched. He also noticed that Davos seemed able to heal people suffering from the disease. In February 1865 the first two patients, two German men, arrived in Davos and were cured. Originally Spengler restricted the cure to the summer, fearing the winter was too cold and damp. But later, patients took the fresh air and sun at midday in winter. Spengler's cure remains controversial, with medical science still unable to explain whether the sunshine and fresh air of Davos did or did not have an effect on tuberculosis.

4. The tubercles, or tumours, were either closed, like a closed wound, or if the disease was more serious, open. If open, the danger of contagion was considerable as the bacillus could escape from the wound and into the lungs and then be coughed or sneezed out into the open air where it could infect another body.

5. The pneumothorax was an operation to pump air into the space in the body wall between the pleura of the thorax and of the lungs. The air was pumped in through a blunt needle.

6. Streptomycin is an antibiotic that is effective against some groups of disease-producing bacteria that are immune to penicillin.

7. Davos is still Switzerland's largest health resort, however. It treats some 380,000 patients a year in sanatoria and clinics for skin allergies as well as bronchial and asthmatic difficulties.

Chapter 8

SWISS POLITICS: REFERENDUMS AND CONSENSUS

In 1984 Elisabeth Kopp became the first woman to be elected to the Swiss government's seven-strong Federal Council – the cabinet of the government and the pinnacle of a political career in Switzerland.

A lawyer and a member of the Free Democratic Party, Kopp was voted the most popular politician in Switzerland while she was in office. However, less than five years after her rise to power she had provoked Switzerland's severest domestic political crisis since the Second World War. She admitted telling her husband in a telephone conversation that a company of which he was a director was linked to an investigation by federal authorities for suspected money laundering. Kopp resigned and became the first minister in Swiss history to face criminal charges.

The so-called Kopp Affair shook the public's faith in their politicians. Its aftermath shook their confidence in the whole political system, for, after Kopp stepped down, a parliamentary inquiry into the justice ministry and the circumstances surrounding her resignation announced that Swiss police had built up a huge number of detailed secret files on one-sixth of the country's population since the early years of the Cold War.

Elisabeth Kopp has remained controversial. While some are convinced she was the victim of political enemies who exploited her indiscretion to the full, others say her acquittal by the Federal Court in 1990 made a laughing stock of Swiss justice.[1]

The Kopp Affair stands at the beginning of a gathering sense of crisis in the Swiss political system in recent years. Opinion polls have recorded sharp falls in the public's confidence in government abilities; Berne's recommendations in a number of important referendums have been ignored by the electorate; and discussions on how to reform political institutions have remained inconclusive.[2]

The crisis has also brought into question the broad social and political consensus that is the bedrock of Switzerland's post-World War Two success. Early in 1994 the economics minister, Jean-Pascal Delamuraz, complained: 'The ability of industry and government to come together and achieve a compromise has lessened. There is also a lack of dialogue between business and politicians. The social peace, which used to be a major attraction and achievement of Switzerland, is also changing. If voters are called to the ballot box four times to vote on the question of animal experiments then this is not exactly boosting confidence in our political institutions. This simply leads to great investment insecurities for our chemical industry.'[3]

In this chapter Elisabeth Kopp talks of the crisis facing the Swiss political system and of her view of the Kopp Affair.

Notes

1. Elisabeth Kopp's husband has not avoided controversy either. In 1991 a Zurich court found Elisabeth Kopp's husband, Hans, guilty of fraud and falsification of documents. Hans Kopp appealed and took the case to Switzerland's highest court, the Federal Court in Lausanne, which confirmed the ruling in June 1994. Hans Kopp said soon after that the decision was politically motivated.

2. Public opinion polls, held a number of times a year, show that since 1991 the public has lost trust in the Swiss government after 15 years of almost uninterrupted confidence in Berne's abilities (Schloeth, 1994, p. 10).

3. Jean-Pascal Delamuraz to *Schweizerische Handelszeitung*, on 27 January 1994. The Swiss last voted in a referendum on whether to restrict experiments on animals for medical research in February 1992.

THE KOPP AFFAIR

Elisabeth Kopp

Elisabeth Kopp, 57, enters the room quietly, almost furtively, opening and closing the door slowly and carefully. A handbag hangs
from her forearm and she is conservatively dressed in a two-
piece suit. Her short brown hair is greying slightly. Her walk is
controlled but fragile, as if remaining upright requires a lot of
energy. She sits upright at the table, talks precisely and in a low
tone. Occasionally, she seems to forget and her face shows enjoyment at discussion and debate. Once, uncharacteristically, she
jumps up and walks around the table with a book to illustrate a
point.

Even though it has only existed for 35 years, the 'magic formula'[1]
is now at the core of the Swiss political system. It was first introduced in 1959. For the second half of the nineteenth century the
Bundesrat (Federal Council) was controlled by the Free Democratic
Party (FDP), which also held an absolute majority in the lower
house of parliament. The growth of the Social Democratic Party
(SPS) and the election of Ernst Nobs as the first Social Democratic
minister to the *Bundesrat* in the 1943 coalition was a small revolution and broke the hold of the FDP and the bourgeois parties,
which by then together made up the majority. Together the FDP,
the Christian People's Party (CVP), the Swiss People's Party (SVP)
and the SPS forged an uneasy coalition, and then in 1959 agreed
on the 'magic formula'. It was an agreement for compromise and
has dominated Swiss political culture in the post-War period.

The 'magic formula' was partly a reaction to Switzerland's
system of direct democracy.[2] With the Social Democrats in the

governing coalition it was felt it would make sense for the parties to have already achieved a certain consensus on legislative proposals in the *Bundesrat* rather than have a more confrontational process which would have led to individual parties resorting to referendums as a political weapon. That would have made the country difficult to govern. For many years this system functioned rather well, particularly during the economic boom when there was a large cake to be divided and when politics worked on the basis of one hand washing the other.

The fact that the economy is now in difficulty, that unemployment is very high for Switzerland and the state deep in debt is undoubtedly one of the main reasons why the 'magic formula' is now being questioned. Once the cake gets smaller the battles over the size of the pieces becomes much more bitter. The 'magic formula' is also under pressure because the range of common interests among the parties has slowly but surely been exhausted. The tendency in recent years for a coalition party, perhaps driven by its members at the grass roots, to break away and organise a referendum despite the 'magic formula' forces you to wonder whether all this compromising make sense. It has been the left wing above all that again and again has broken ranks, for example over military issues.

But even though the 'magic formula' seems to be being questioned at the moment this does not mean it's necessary to throw it all overboard. One would need to know in very concrete terms what consequences this would have, for example for the distribution of top appointments in the administration. It's not good enough for the coalition parties to hold internal party discussions on the future of the 1959 formula and then come out saying they are simply going to keep an eye on the issue. There is no clear analysis of what an abandonment of the 'magic formula' would mean in real terms. It's not the kind of decision one can make casually, on the back of an envelope.

Of course, part of the reason for this is that the 'magic formula' is a nice cosy arrangement for the coalition parties. It saves them from having to compete and campaign against each other for seats in the *Bundesrat*. Their interests are secure in a cartel structure, a typically Swiss arrangement, and so they've no interest in abandoning the 'magic formula'.

For me a much more important issue than the 1959 agreement

is how to raise the quality of leadership in the government – raise the quality of the seven ministers in the *Bundesrat*. At present we are in a vicious circle. It is quite understandable that the job of a minister is no longer very attractive in Switzerland. The job is encumbered with so many chains that it simply does not appeal to a dynamic person. Here as soon as someone is dynamic, efficient and achieves things they encounter opposition, because people are simply not used to this. Promotion depends more upon membership of a clique than on merit. And so we have people of average ability both in parliament and in the government and these people produce legislation of only average quality and, consequently, the quality of the political leadership of the government has suffered. Qualified and able people see this and are therefore even less willing to serve in politics. That is the downward spiral we are in today.

If only the parliament would work more efficiently, effectively and urgently then it would be able to cut its workload in half. Discussion is the work of the parliament, but that doesn't mean it's necessary for almost everyone in parliament to give their opinion in a debate, especially if they have the same view as the majority. Similarly with motions in the parliament – a lot of time could be saved if parliamentarians first checked with the relevant ministry to see whether a motion makes sense or not. I remember when I was in the *Nationalrat* (lower house of parliament) how all too often parliamentarians would come to me for my signature in support of a motion and I would ask: 'Have you checked with the ministry what the situation is at the moment?' And they would say: 'We don't need to, we need a motion.'

One aspect of Swiss politics that is often criticised is the link between parliament and business. As in the army we also have a militia parliament and not a parliament of professional full-time politicians, and a large proportion of these members of parliament are directors on company boards.[3] Many say this must lead to conflicts of interest. But I don't agree, I see it more as an advantage than a danger, as long as the interests involved are fully declared and everyone knows who is representing what interests. If someone has an influential position in the economy through a directorship and at the same time is a member of the lower house or the upper house, this can be of benefit for the parliament and for the country. He or she has a whole range of experience, knowledge or technical expertise to offer the parliament that a professional politician, who has spent his or her whole life in politics, probably would not have. But everyone has to know very precisely who is representing which interests.

Also the fact that many members of parliament are anchored somewhere in civilian life is positive. Parliamentarians with a civilian career will always have something to fall back on if they are not re-elected, whereas professional politicians will spend a lot more of their time worrying about their re-election. And I say that as a professional politician myself. I trained as a lawyer, I took a career break for a couple of years for the birth and childhood of my daughter and then I became active in local politics in Zumikon.[4] Later when my daughter was older I was elected first as mayor and then subsequently into the national parliament and, finally, into the Swiss government.

But even with more professional politicians in Switzerland you would not be able to change the system of direct democracy – the people's right of referendum and initiative. I don't think it should be changed although sometimes it disappoints me that direct democracy slows politics down so much in Switzerland: a good example is the right of women to vote, which was rejected at a national referendum in 1959 but was then passed in 1971.[5] In other countries, where change is not so closely controlled by the electorate, this kind of reform could easily have been introduced much earlier by a simple act of government and parliament, but in Switzerland it needed a couple of referendums and therefore took much longer.

Direct democracy may also expose the population to demagogues. If an issue is very complex people may not fully understand it and they become more susceptible to simplistic demagogic explanations of the issues involved. The vote on the European Economic Area (EEA) is in my opinion a good example of this.[6] I feel concerned if I see and am convinced that people are voting against their best interests. It would obviously have been in the best interests of the Swiss people to join the EEA because it would have given them the economic benefits of access to European markets without the political disadvantages of altering the system of direct democracy. But the campaign by those opposed to EEA membership was so simplistic in its warnings – that Swiss neutrality and direct democracy were threatened, that foreigners would take Swiss jobs and that Switzerland would lose its economic independence to bureaucrats in Brussels – that a balanced decision was not possible.

By the time the Swiss people are ready to join the EEA it probably won't exist any more, or will be worthless because most of its members will already have joined the European Union.

Direct democracy is the bedrock of the Swiss political system. It is what holds a highly federal country of 26 cantons and four languages and cultures together. The average Swiss may not even vote in ninety-nine referendums, but at the hundredth he'll be there with his ballot paper. And if you even scratch at his political rights he'll be climbing the barricades immediately. The system is irreversible in my opinion. And the more people lose confidence in the government and the politicians in general, the less they will be willing to renounce even part of their political rights.

But despite all this concern for democracy it is undeniable that the Swiss state resorted to spying on its own citizens without sufficient legal basis for any such activity. It is not the case, as some have claimed, that the secret files on people living in Switzerland were compiled by the police without the knowledge or the approval of parliament.[7] The secret files were started during the Cold War with the full knowledge and approval of parliament and the government, and were then continued without clear guidelines from parliament or the government. The files developed a kind of life of their own. The police continued putting them together and they were not rigorously controlled by the executive or the legislature.

It is true, of course, that many states – probably all states – have files on some of their citizens. And it is also true that during the Cold War secret surveillance was a very important and legitimate part of counter-espionage activities against the Eastern Bloc. But this does not justify the uncontrolled proliferation of surveillance, telephone tapping, monitoring of post,[8] and so on that went on.

Most of the files were kept by the federal police. I think a lot of the files were stored in cellars at the federal police building because they were running out of space in their offices. About two-thirds of the files covered foreigners living in Switzerland, another large share Swiss who had contacts with foreigners and the rest Swiss citizens. There were files on 70 members of parliament, including the then justice minister. About 80 per cent of the files had not been updated for over twenty years. I don't know if there was a file on me; I have not looked.

But the issue of the files was also blown out of proportion.

After I had stepped down there was a parliamentary inquiry into the justice ministry and the federal prosecutor's office to clarify the circumstances of my resignation. The inquiry took up the issue of the files and made a big political and media event out of them, even though another parliamentary committee had just completed a critical report on the files a year earlier. The files were certainly outrageous, but one should not compare them with the situation elsewhere, for example in East Germany. People were not systematically disadvantaged because of the information in their files in Switzerland. If there were even one case in which someone had suffered because of their file then that would truly be tragic.

In many ways the 'Kopp Affair' showed very clearly what is wrong with the Swiss political system. Many close observers of Swiss politics are convinced that the 'Kopp Affair' could and should have been avoided.

It's difficult to have been so high, so successful in politics and then to have fallen so low. My father reminded me at the time of the fable of Polycrates, who provoked the envy of the gods with his success and they then destroyed him.[9] Maybe there was something in what he said. I suppose I had had a lot of luck in my life; I was successful with almost everything I put my hand to: in sport – I was quite successful with ice skating – in my studies and in my family life. I am happily married and we have a wonderful daughter and two grandchildren. I was also, essentially, successful in politics. Thirteen years after women got the right to vote in Switzerland I was the first woman to be elected to the Swiss government. There most of my proposals were approved and the people I worked with were very motivated. That was part of the success and when the fall then came it was correspondingly harder.

I was practically forced to leave my offices in Berne after my resignation on 12 January through a back door and not one of my former colleagues in the government has thought of inquiring after me since. And that hurts.

The so-called information that my personal assistant Katharina Schoop gave to me on 27 October 1988 – in fact it was nothing more than a false rumour – was the first information I saw linking Shakarchi Trading, the company where my husband was vice president of the board, to money laundering. I immediately called my husband to ask him to step down from the board. Mr Shakarchi had already informed my husband on 21 October at the company's annual general meeting that if he wished to step down, if the rumours surrounding him and the company did not subside, the board would understand this. During our telephone conversation my husband calmed me and assured me that the company was clean and above suspicion,[10] but said that if I insisted he was prepared to step down that day. I said I would prefer that and told him he could get any further information he needed from my assistant. My famous phone call was not a warning, as it was immediately interpreted, nor was I acting as a loving wife. As a member of the government I simply could not afford to be in a situation where the name of my husband was linked with money laundering, particularly when at the time I was preparing a law on money laundering.

You know the French expression – *le mari est toujours le dernier informé*? Well, that was the case here. All around me journalists were talking about this suspected link, and an official at the federal police knew about rumours of a possible link and had also informed Dr Renate Schwob, in the justice ministry, who was a legal specialist on money laundering. Schwob in turn informed my assistant, Schoop, who was not an official of my ministry. If I had had any idea this so-called information was from my own ministry I would probably have acted differently – talked to the federal police, or something.

But since I did not know that and thought the so-called information was from outside my department – Schoop was a friend of the secretary of the Swiss Bankers' Association and often gave me information from that source – I thought it made sense for my husband to step down from the board to avoid difficulties for me. I was due to be elected vice president of Switzerland in December 1988 and his resignation seemed an ideal way to bring some of the rumour-mongering to an end. Furthermore, it can hardly be said that I gave my husband an advantage by passing on allegedly confidential information because, if there had been any truth in the allegations of money laundering against Shakarchi, he would still have been liable to prosecution even after he had resigned.

I have been asking myself over the last years who was behind my fall from power, who wanted to engineer it. Some people who have closely followed the whole issue are convinced that such a continuous and long-term campaign directed against me through my husband was not coincidental. Somewhere there must have been someone who was opposed to me or to what I was doing. It may have had something to do with the legislation I was working on to control money laundering that may have annoyed certain interests – that's one possibility. There was also envy because I was considered to be the leading politician in the government.

It was noticeable how little political support I had from my party or other ministerial colleagues. If my party had supported me and said: 'We'll battle this through together,' I might have had more courage to fight on rather than resign. I was not the kind of politician who bends with the wind and I paid for that. I had annoyed the left with measures to accelerate the procedure for deciding on whether to grant political asylum, and I had annoyed financial interests with tough measures aimed at controlling money laundering and a law against pornography.

The so-called Kopp Affair still occupies people's minds in Switzerland and there are two clear schools of thought on it. One strand of opinion is voiced among politicians and journalists who all say: 'For God's sake, no comeback by Kopp.' And the politicians, particularly in my own party, react extremely nervously if I have a public engagement anywhere. The other school of thought is encouraging – almost daily I receive letters of support from people all over Switzerland and people stop me in the street and express their support for me.[11]

Notes

1. The 'magic formula' is the 1959 agreement between the four parties of the government coalition to divide the seven seats of the Federal Council, the executive cabinet of the Swiss government, among themselves according to a fixed formula. The Christian People's Party (CVP), the FDP and the SPS have two seats each in the cabinet, and the Swiss People's Party (SVP), which originally represented agrarian interests, has one seat. The coalition also has an unwritten rule that two to three of the cabinet seats must be reserved for candidates from French-speaking Switzerland. The members of the cabinet serve for four years and can be re-elected any number of times by parliament. In the past, members of the *Bundesrat* have served on average for ten years.

2. The Swiss constitution grants citizens extensive democratic powers. Citizens wishing to propose or initiate legislation must collect a minimum of 100,000 signatures to call a national vote on the initiative. Changes of the constitution by the government face an obligatory plebiscite, while any other legislation by Berne that people disagree with can be forced to a referendum

with the collection of 50,000 signatures of opposition. Initiatives and referendums can also be organised at the cantonal and communal level. Swiss citizens vote four times a year in federal plebiscites on issues ranging from the country's membership of international organisations to the legalisation of casinos.

3. In the 1991–95 parliament more than half of the members of the lower house of parliament (*Nationalrat*) and close to three-quarters of the members of the upper house of parliament (*Staenderat*) held at least one company directorship (see Appendix to Verzeichnis der Verwaltungsraete, 1994).

4. Zumikon is a commune on the outskirts of Zurich.

5. The 1971 referendum enfranchised women for all federal elections. However, a number of individual cantons continued to deny women the vote at cantonal level. The last of these was the small eastern Swiss canton of Appenzell Innerrhoden which first allowed women to vote in 1990.

6. In December 1992, after one of the most bitterly-fought referendum campaigns in Swiss history, the Swiss voted against joining the EEA.

7. In 1989 a parliamentary committee charged with investigating the justice ministry following the resignation of Elisabeth Kopp announced that Swiss police had compiled files on around 900,000 Swiss citizens and foreigners living in Switzerland. It said that the files were used to vet people applying for public office. Much of the information in the files was unverified and taken from informers. The Swiss government said soon after that anyone wishing to see the entries on their files could do so and that superfluous files would be destroyed. According to media reports at the time one woman's file said she had written a letter to a newspaper protesting against the sacking of a radio employee. Another woman's file noted she was in regular contact with the Soviet Union, but did not mention that this was a regular part of her job as a representative of Swiss youth organisations. Member of parliament Max Duenki was secretly watched and his file noted that he had been visited by the secretary of the East German embassy carrying a folder and that Duenki later accompanied the secretary to his car in the car park. It did not mention that Duenki had visited East Germany with an official delegation and that the secretary was calling to hear his views on the visit and to present him with a book on housing in East Germany. The Basle police chief said in early 1990 that 70 per cent of the 50,000 files stored in Basle could be destroyed without entailing any threat to security. (See Reuters news agency reports from November 1989 to February 1990.)

8. The parliamentary committee reported in June 1990 that Swiss postal officials had secretly copied telegrams sent to East Germany between 1969 and 1986 and passed the copies to Swiss intelligence services. Swiss customs officers also reported to the police on Swiss citizens' mail (Reuters news agency, 1 June 1990).

9. According to Greek legend Polycrates was the tyrant of the Greek island

of Xenos near the Persian coast. He was very rich and successful and a friend told him he should give some of his wealth away. Following his friend's advice Polycrates threw his seal ring into the sea, but a fish brought it back to him the next day. The friend saw this as a bad omen and said Polycrates was damned. Soon after Polycrates was killed by the Persians.

10. A year-long investigation of Shakarchi Trading by Swiss authorities failed to yield any grounds for charges.

11. In September 1989 authorities charged Elisabeth Kopp, Katharina Schoop and Renate Schwob of breaching official secrecy. After a trial at the Federal Court in Lausanne in February 1990 Kopp and Schwob were acquitted, but Kopp was required to pay some court costs. Schwob was awarded compensation. Schoop was found guilty of making legal errors, but not punished.

Chronology of the 'Kopp Affair'

- 2 October 1984: Elisabeth Kopp first woman to be elected to *Bundesrat*.
- 21 July 1986: Elisabeth Kopp charges Federal Public Prosecutor Paolo Bernasconi with the drafting of a law against money laundering.
- 26 August 1988: Swiss magazine reports Hans Kopp evaded paying millions of francs' worth of taxes.
- 8 September 1988: Official in federal police office makes notes in files for the federal prosecutor, Rudolf Gerber, in the trial of the Magharian brothers, two Lebanese accused of being members of an international drug ring and of having laundered over a billion dollars through Switzerland. The two Lebanese were linked to Shakarchi Trading Co., where Hans Kopp was a director and vice chairman.
- 17 October 1988: Official in federal police gives file notes and a confidential report to Dr Renate Schwob, a legal specialist in the justice ministry.
- 21 October 1988: Hans Kopp informs board of Shakarchi Trading that he reserves the right to step down with immediate effect if rumours surrounding himself and the company do not cease.
- 25 October 1988: Schwob shows the file notes to Katharina Schoop, personal assistant to Elisabeth Kopp. Schoop informs the general secretary of the justice ministry.
- 27 October 1988: Schoop informs Elisabeth Kopp that Shakarchi Trading is being named in association with a money laundering case. Elisabeth Kopp calls her husband and asks him to step down from the board of Shakarchi Trading. Hans Kopp later calls Schoop for more details.
- 4 November 1988: A Swiss daily reports an alleged large money laundering scandal and names Shakarchi Trading and its former vice president Hans Kopp.
- 7 November 1988: General secretary of the justice ministry informs Elisabeth Kopp that some of Schoop's information is from federal police sources, within the justice ministry.

- 9 November 1988: Elisabeth Kopp informs the cabinet about the charges against the two Magharian brothers and their impending trial but does not mention the telephone conversation with her husband.
- 10 November 1988: General secretary of the justice ministry informs federal attorney and other senior officials of the telephone conversations on 27 October.
- 7 December 1988: Elisabeth Kopp is elected vice president of Swiss confederation with 165 out of 238 votes.
- 9 December 1988: Swiss daily reports that the justice ministry is conducting an internal investigation to check an information leak. Elisabeth Kopp informs the public and the cabinet of the two telephone conversations.
- 12 December 1988: Elisabeth Kopp announces her resignation, to take effect at the end of February.
- 12 January 1989: Elisabeth Kopp announces her resignation with immediate effect.
- 20 September 1989: Extraordinary federal public prosecutor brings charges against Elisabeth Kopp, Schoop and Schwob of breaching official secrecy.
- 19–23 February 1990: Elisabeth Kopp and Schwob found not guilty of breaching official secrecy. Elisabeth Kopp must pay some court costs, however, while Schwob ordered to pay compensation. Schoop found guilty of making legal errors, but not punished.

Chapter 9

REFUGEES IN SWITZERLAND

The image of Switzerland's national flag, the white cross on a red background, is indelibly imprinted on the consciousness of the twentieth-century world as a symbol of neutrality and of a haven for the persecuted. Indeed the International Committee of the Red Cross, which was founded in Geneva in 1863 to protect the victims of armed conflict, simply reversed the colours of the Swiss flag when designing its own, in honour of the host nation.

The Swiss can point to an illustrious list of people who have sought refuge in their country. At the end of the seventeenth century tens of thousands of Huguenots fled France, where Calvinism had been forbidden, to Switzerland. In the nineteenth century two of the most important forces behind Italian republicanism, Giuseppe Mazzini and Giuseppe Garibaldi, both spent time in Switzerland to escape persecution at home. The Russian anarchist Mikhail Bakhunin died in Switzerland and is buried in Berne. And in the early twentieth century Vladimir Lenin lived in Switzerland from 1914 to 1917 before being smuggled back into Russia in a sealed train across Germany.

However, after the First World War the practice changed. The Swiss, who had until then been ready to accept almost anyone into their country, began to become more particular. Economic pressures and the threat of foreigners taking Swiss jobs dictated that not all foreigners be allowed into the country. For the first time Swiss authorities began the registration of foreigners living in Switzerland. This policy reached its logical but terrible conclusion first with the restrictions imposed on foreign Jews trying to enter the country in the late 1930s and finally with the sealing of Swiss borders at the height of the Final Solution in Nazi Germany. Fears that millions of Jewish refugees would destabilise the Swiss labour market combined with a latent anti-Semitism ensured that thousands of Jews were turned back to face almost certain death during the Second World War.

In this chapter Mario Gattiker, head of the legal department at the Swiss branch of the international Caritas charity group, describes Switzerland's policies towards refugees in the twentieth century and explains how the concern for Swiss jobs was often of more importance than the provision of a safe haven for the persecuted.

Rakra Tethong, one of the first Tibetan refugees to arrive in Switzerland following the crushing of an uprising in Tibet by Chinese forces in 1959, gives the other side of the refugee story – the life of a refugee in Switzerland.

REFUGEES OR JOBS

Mario Gattiker

Mario Gattiker, 38, is informally dressed in jeans, open-necked shirt and jacket. His office is on the third floor of an old house in central Lucerne. We climb a narrow staircase and sit at a small, round, glass-topped table. The office is lined with bookshelves filled with books and papers.

He has been involved in refugee affairs for nearly ten years, working first for the charity of the Protestant Churches of Switzerland in Berne and then for Caritas from 1989. Gattiker gives asylum seekers legal advice and his department sends representatives to observe the interrogation of asylum seekers by Swiss officials. Swiss asylum law requires that every questioning of an asylum seeker be attended by a representative of an independent charity to ensure the proceedings are fair.

Despite its international image of neutrality and support for the world's persecuted, Switzerland was not traditionally a country that offered refuge. From the middle of the nineteenth century until the start of the First World War there was really no such thing as a refugee in Switzerland because foreigners were more or less free to enter and settle in Switzerland (*Niederlassungsfreiheit*). Only people who were considered a threat to the state or criminals were not allowed into the country. But apart from these there was general free immigration for people from a number of countries which had signed treaties with Switzerland. So whether you were moving to Switzerland because you liked the Alps or because you were afraid of being locked up in your home country did not make any difference – you were free to come and go.

The First World War and the economic crisis after 1918 changed all this. For the first time Switzerland introduced tough restrictions on other nationals. Visas were required for foreigners entering the country, there were stringent border controls, foreigners living in Switzerland had to register themselves with their local authorities and a federal foreigners' police force was set up. For the first time policy towards immigration was dictated by whether foreigners entering the country would threaten Swiss jobs. And this raised the problem of political refugees – whether there was an obligation to let people in because they were fleeing persecution even though they might be a strain on the labour market.

Of course, it is true that there is a certain humanitarian tradition in Switzerland, a tradition of sheltering refugees and the persecuted. In the late seventeenth century thousands of Huguenots fled Catholic persecution in France and sought refuge in western Switzerland, with many settling there. And of course there are the famous cases of Lenin and James Joyce.[1]

But if you look at the last two centuries then you see that Swiss policy on taking in foreigners and also refugees was mainly a matter of economic considerations. When labour was in short supply, the borders were open and there was free immigration, as in the nineteenth century and also later after the Second World War in the 1960s and 1970s. Once Swiss jobs came under threat from foreign workers the borders were slammed shut and refugees found a less warm welcome, as after the First World War and in the late 1980s and early 1990s.

This policy went completely out of control and became inhuman before and during the Second World War. At this time the Swiss government, in a shameful decision, turned Jews fleeing Nazi persecution back at the border and later closed its borders altogether – fearing, among other things, that the country would be flooded with Jews who would be an unbearable burden on the labour market.[2] The policy probably sent several thousands of Jews to their deaths in the concentration camps.

After the Second World War an embarrassed Swiss government tried to make amends by setting political asylum as a strategic goal. A kind of state maxim was passed in 1957. But it retained the granting of asylum as a decision for the state – at the state's discretion – and did not see asylum as a right of the persecuted individual. The view now was that Switzerland should become more generous in granting political asylum. During the Cold War we had waves of refugees escaping Eastern Europe who were given asylum in Switzerland – from Hungary in 1956, from Czechoslovakia in 1968, and from Poland in 1980. And from outside Europe there was Tibet in 1960, Chile in 1973 and also refugees from the Vietnam War.

But although the Swiss government was concerned about its image after the treatment of the Jews during the Second World War, the economic aspect had not been forgotten. The 1950s, 1960s and 1970s were years of economic growth for Switzerland, even of economic boom, and the Swiss never had any reason to fear that the refugees or the thousands of foreigners who were allowed into the country on short-term visas would deprive Swiss citizens of a job. There was also an ideological component. With the exception of Chile, the refugees in this period were all from the communist or the socialist world. Granting asylum to refugees from these countries was not politically controversial at home because the right wing was happy to display any proof of the bankruptcy of communism and the Eastern Bloc.

It is true that there was controversy in the 1960s over the issue of *Ueberfremdung* (excessive foreign immigration) and a series of referendums was held on the question of whether Switzerland should restrict the number of foreigners working in the country. But this animosity was directed only at foreign workers, mainly from southern Europe, who were employed in Switzerland in menial jobs in hotels, restaurants and on the streets, and not at refugees seeking asylum.[3] Switzerland has a relatively high proportion of foreigners in its population, about 20 per cent, and these referendums were really an indication that the integration of people from different cultures and with different languages is not easy. But asylum seekers from communist countries were never a domestic political issue.

So by the late 1970s Switzerland could feel relatively proud of its asylum record. To the government the problem seemed manageable without posing a threat to Swiss jobs. Political refugees were seen to be almost exclusively an Eastern European and communist phenomenon. A re-worked asylum law was passed in 1979 which laid down a clear definition of who qualified as a refugee. The definition was broader and more liberal than the definition in the Geneva Convention on Refugees: refugees were foreigners who had genuine grounds for fearing persecution or the suffering of serious disadvantage because of their race, religion, membership of a group, nationality or domestic political views. Serious disadvantages were threat to body, life and freedom as well as measures that exerted an intolerable psychological pressure.

But just at this time, when things seemed to be going so well for Swiss asylum policy, the nature of the refugee problem changed dramatically. Huge numbers of refugees from the South seeking asylum in the North suddenly undermined the carefully-prepared new asylum law which had assumed asylum seekers only came from the totalitarian regimes of Eastern Europe and not in very large numbers. Until 1981 Switzerland had received between 1,000 and 2,000 appeals for political asylum a year and had granted most if not all of these. After 1981 the numbers leapt, reaching a peak in 1991 with over 41,000 appeals. They have fallen back to between 20,000 and 30,000 a year.

This was a problem for all of western Europe – all of the Western world in fact – but Switzerland had relatively more appeals for asylum per capita because it paid higher wages than other European countries and was therefore much more attractive to Third World refugees. Germany was very quick to introduce restrictions and asylum seekers were banned from working there. But in Switzerland there was still a labour shortage and a lot of demand for short-term work in the tourist industry, so asylum seekers could continue to take jobs until a three-month ban was introduced in 1986.

But although Switzerland did not start restricting asylum seekers from finding jobs until later, the potential danger of a wave of refugees was recognised and the approval rates for political asylum dropped significantly. Between 2 and 5 per cent of asylum seekers from Sri Lanka are now granted asylum, which is far too low given the level of persecution suffered by many people in that country. In 1979 close to 100 per cent of all appeals for asylum were approved; by 1982 or 1983 this had dropped to around 15 per cent. And then by 1991, when we reached the peak of appeals, the approvals rate fell to its lowest ever – 2.4 per cent. This coincided with a deep economic recession in which Swiss unemployment rose to its highest levels since the Second World War. So we had a situation in which the more asylum seekers there were, the more restricted the granting of political asylum became. In 1991 and other years when the number of people given asylum was very low, there were undoubtedly many whose appeals would have justified refugee status but who did not get it.

You can see how flexible the state's criteria for granting asylum are if you compare the different assessments by various European countries of whether countries are classified as safe or not for persecuted minorities. Germany for a long time considered Sri Lanka to be unsafe for Tamils and gave asylum to practically all Tamils who appealed in Germany. In Switzerland, however, the rate was much lower. In France roughly half of all Kurds who appeal for asylum are recognised as refugees, but in Switzerland in the second half of the 1980s this rate was only 3 to 5 per cent. It is now much higher, however.

The Swiss government's refugee policy is wrong in relation to Tamils from Sri Lanka, Kurds from east Turkey and the Kosovo Albanians.[4] People from those countries should be given at least a provisional right to stay until the situations in their countries have stabilised. These countries are not safe for the people who are trying to flee them. You don't need to check the individual stories of people from these countries appealing for asylum; they should be given at least a temporary group asylum as long as they are not criminal. As far as the Tamils are concerned Switzerland is the first country that has decided to repatriate Tamils by force, which is something it has been trying to do for some time.[5] In Germany a number of the state governments have granted Kosovo Albanians a blanket asylum without the individuals involved even having to prove they have been individually persecuted.

Although in broad terms Germany, France and Switzerland use the same criteria to decide whether a foreigner is a refugee or not the individual governments come to very different conclusions, and this leaves a lot of scope for authorities to adjust their refugee policy to the needs and state of their home countries and their home economies.

Notes

1. Vladimir Lenin, already an active and recognised Russian revolutionary, lived in exile in Switzerland between 1914 and 1917. He returned in a sealed train across Germany to lead the Bolshevik Revolution in 1917. The Irish author, James Joyce, lived in Zurich on a number of occasions. But the last

time he entered the country in 1940, weeks before his death and fleeing the Nazi advance in France, the Swiss foreigners' police at first tried to stop him on the grounds that he would compete with Swiss authors.

2. For more details on Swiss policy towards foreign Jews during the Second World War see chapter 1, Switzerland and the Jews.

3. A number of initiatives organised in the 1960s and 1970s, which came to national referendums, were aimed at imposing legal limits on the number of foreigners allowed to live in Switzerland. The most well-known of these was the Schwarzenbach Initiative, which was narrowly rejected in June 1970, but some 46 per cent of the population had voted in favour of the proposed controls. A number of other initiatives to limit the number of foreigners living in Switzerland, including one proposing a halving of the foreign population already living in Switzerland in the space of six years, were also rejected.

4. In 1993 around 100 Albanian asylum seekers from the Serbian province of Kosovo were denied political asylum in Switzerland and Swiss authorities ordered them to leave the country by September. Swiss church and other charity and relief organisations, including Caritas, said the decision to repatriate the people was wrong and they should at least be allowed to stay temporarily until the situation in Kosovo had stabilised. Swiss and international relief organisations say that the Serbs are systematically persecuting Albanians in Kosovo. Thirteen Protestant and five Catholic churches in Berne took the Kosovo Albanians into 'church asylum'. Berne police said they would carry out the expulsions but promised they would not resort to dragging the asylum seekers from the churches. Swiss authorities have since, however, had to postpone the planned repatriations as Macedonia, which was previously prepared to act as transit country for the Kosovo Albanians, has withdrawn its cooperation.

5. Switzerland on 13 January 1994 was the first west European country to sign an agreement with Sri Lanka on the forced repatriation of Tamils whose appeals for asylum had been rejected. The agreement with Sri Lanka guarantees that Tamils will not be forced to return to any combat zones and provides for camps to be set up by the Sri Lankan government and Sri Lankan Red Cross in which those repatriated will be able to stay until they find permanent homes. There are some 18,000 Tamils living in Switzerland without residence permits. Around 6,000 of these have been given the right to stay in Switzerland because they have been in the country for more than four years. The remainder must wait for a decision on their appeals for political asylum and if these are negative they will be sent back to Sri Lanka. Since the early 1980s around 200 Tamils have been recognised as political refugees by Swiss authorities.

THE TIBETAN REFUGEE

Rakra Tethong

Rakra Tethong looks like a Tibetan monk. He is 72 years old, has a large bald head, big, protruding ears and round, brown, twinkling eyes. His figure is slight, he smokes a pipe and speaks slowly, almost haltingly, often repeating himself. 'Yeesss!!' he confirms when one has understood something he says. He talks in the lounge of the apartment where he and his wife live. The home is furnished in Western style and Rakra Tethong wears tight-fitting Western clothes. A copy of a book on Tibetan Buddhism lies on the coffee table in front of him.

'When I was a child, I was two or three years old, an eastern Tibetan monastery wrote to the Dalai Lama saying that I (Tethong's son) was one of the reincarnations of an earlier lama and that when I was old enough they wanted to take me into the monastery and educate me to become a lama. Education in a monastery in Tibet was the only chance of a good education; often it was a good chance for poor boys. If I had not been recognised as a reincarnation I would not have been able to study at the monastery.

'So the idea was that I would become a lama. In Tibet I would be called Rakra, which is the name of the lama of whom I am a reincarnation. My father did not like the idea at all. He didn't believe I could be the reincarnation of a lama because I was the son of a man who had killed Chinese in battle – my father was a military officer. Of course he was happy that I could study religion but he was not happy that I was to become a lama, not happy at all.

'I was educated in Drepung monastery, which was one of the biggest at that time with some three thousand teachers and three and a half thousand students. When I was 25 I became a lama. But soon after I decided to go to India to learn Sanskrit.

'So I was in India for about eleven years. I studied near Calcutta and was later appointed assistant lecturer at a university near Poona. Then about 1955 the Indian government started Tibetan broadcasts from All-India Radio and they asked me to join them. At that time there were very few Tibetans who spoke Hindi, English or any other foreign language. I gave mostly cultural talks. Also I had to earn money because following the Communist Chinese occupation of Tibet in 1950 I was cut off from my money in Tibet.'

In 1960 Rakra Tethong arrived in Switzerland as one of the first Tibetans ever to enter the country. He had come to look after exiled Tibetan children and spent the next 27 years in a small eastern Swiss village set up for foreign refugee children after the Second World War. The Pestalozzi Children's Village, a collection of 15 wooden houses for children of 25 different nationalities, lies at the top of a steep climb in the undulating hills near the village of Trogen in the canton of Appenzell Ausserrhoden, overlooking Lake Constanz.[1]

We arrived here on 17 August 1960 and at that time there were no Tibetans in Switzerland. It was not my aim in life then to teach children in Switzerland; my main interest was Indian Buddhist literature. But life took another course. While I was working for the All-India Radio the Dalai Lama and many Tibetans fled to India from Tibet after the Chinese invasion.[2] And then at the end of 1959 the head of the British commission in Tibet, Mr Richardson, wrote me a letter and told me about the Pestalozzi Children's Village here in Switzerland and asked me whether I would like to look after some Tibetan children in the village. I was not very keen: I had no experience with children and little experience of Western culture; and anyway I wanted to concentrate on my studies of Indian Buddhist literature. I hoped to go to England to do some research.

But then the elder brother of the Dalai Lama,[3] who was living in the United States, asked me to accept the offer. He said I could go with my wife and we would have 20 Tibetan children to look after. Still I resisted due to my lack of experience with children and of Western culture. The Dalai Lama's brother mentioned my name to the Pestalozzi Children's Village and they asked me through Mr Richardson, who came to India soon after. He told me how badly these children needed parents. I had heard how the children who had fled Tibet were living in very bad conditions in a children's village in Dharamsala. And so finally I agreed. I resigned from All-India Radio and hurried to Dharamsala. The conditions really were terrible. There were some two to three hundred kids living in a small hall. They did not have enough food.

From the beginning in Switzerland we had a lot of trouble adjusting to Western life. We had no experience of what Western life meant. And then we had to educate the Tibetan children. But which way? The traditional Tibetan education is only suitable for children in Tibet who are training to be lamas. I did not want the children to lose touch with Tibetan religious and cultural traditions, but the classical education was not right for Tibetan children who were living in Switzerland and would probably spend their lives working here – and even if not in Switzerland, certainly outside Tibet. I asked the education department of the Tibetan government in exile in Dharamsala to send us school books written in the common spoken language and not in the literary Tibetan that the books were usually written in. But they said I should use the literary language to ensure that it and the cultural traditions were passed on to the next generation. I disagreed. Lots of other countries have been through the same development and switched from a literary language to a spoken language without losing touch with their history and culture. One needs to find links between old and new languages.

Without the books I wanted it was difficult. My main target was to teach the children to speak Tibetan, because through language you can learn a lot. The writing was difficult because we did not have the right materials, so that even if I had wanted my children to learn to write it would not have been possible. I taught Tibetan language, history, geography and some simple religious instruction.

When my wife and I started at Pestalozzi there were 14 different nationalities living there. Each house gave lessons to its own children and taught the children about their national traditions and culture. All ceremonies and festivals were celebrated in the individual houses and that was good for maintaining national traditions. We prayed every morning and before meals. In the morning we prayed for a longer period, about a quarter of an hour or so. I am sure we were not a typical Tibetan community, but at the same time it was not forced – we spoke Tibetan naturally.

However, after ten years it became clear that the educational targets that I and other people in the village had set ourselves could not be met. We could not – or should not – create children who knew all about their own ethnic culture but nothing about the society in which they were living and in which most of them were going to spend their lives. We had to loosen the ties to their cultural roots. We had to. So things in the village were changed and we set up an international house in which children from many different countries were educated together and were prepared for life and jobs in Switzerland.

I left the Children's Village in 1987. In the 27 years we spent there my wife and I brought up four groups of Tibetan children in the village, 44 children in total. I am quite proud that those children can all speak Tibetan. They can't write so well or read so well, but they can talk to other Tibetans and can learn from other Tibetans. My wife still teaches there.

Living in Switzerland has not only helped me understand the West, it has also helped me understand Tibet. People welcomed us in Switzerland when we arrived and this was a great support because it was at the time of the Tibetan people's greatest disaster. Everyone was very sympathetic. Life in the West was not completely new to me – I had had some contacts with Western scholars and many missionaries, so it was not a complete shock. I was not totally ignorant of Western culture, but of course I had no idea of what living in the West was really like.

After a few years in the Children's Village I became a member of the fire brigade in Trogen. I don't think I understood very much of the fire officer's orders because of his strong Appenzell dialect. I think we just communicated by gesture. However, I have to say that I was never made fun of for my mistakes. Everyone was very friendly. The traditions and lifestyle of the Appenzellers have certain similarities with the lifestyle of the Tibetans. They both look after the animals and the fields in basically the same way. In Switzerland the technology is more modern than that in Tibet, of course, but the basic ideas are the same. Also the traditional headdress of Appenzell farmers' women is very similar to the costumes of our traditional Tibetan opera, although the colours are different.

When I first came to Switzerland I thought religion had died out in the West. I was used to daily prayers and to long prayers and neither of these exist here. Church rules and religious practices are also very different here. But gradually I realised that religious values are inherent in the education children get in the schools here. And this is something we Tibetans still have to learn. We have to learn that religious education and education in general is not just for the monks but also for the lay people. I still feel today that we need to pay more attention to the lay people in religious education. The lamas in Tibet remain too élitist.

I have tried many times to persuade the Tibetan government in Dharamsala to produce simple children's books or a newspaper written in the common spoken language instead of the scholarly language, so that ordinary Tibetans would have something to read. Many Tibetans don't agree with me, but I believe that we have to change. The literary language doesn't help the education of the ordinary people. It leaves them uneducated. The language that is taught to the Tibetan children in Dharamsala is mostly the literary language not the spoken language. In Tibet they teach the spoken language in the early school years and then suddenly change and teach the literary language, which children cannot use in daily life since the literary language uses a different vocabulary, conjugations and structure from the ordinary spoken language. In Dharamsala many Tibetan children speak a mixture of Tibetan, Chinese, English and Hindi. So one of the dangers is that we are going to lose the common spoken Tibetan language – even in Tibet the young people speak a mixture of Chinese and Tibetan.

I have written a few children's books for the Tibetan community here using the spoken language and I would like to transcribe Tibetan literature into the common language. Tibetan education is still too élitist. There should be more democracy in Tibet and our people should have a faith which is not divided into religion for the monastery and religion for the people. I don't know to what extent high Tibetan religious circles accept these ideas.

My ideological contribution to the revolution in Tibet is that, before we can successfully throw the Chinese out of Tibet, we need the Tibetan people to be well educated. Tibet needs to make the jump from the Middle Ages into the twentieth century. Over the last few centuries the Tibetan government ignored the Tibetan people and did not worry about their education. Lots of schools for the ordinary people only taught reading and writing and nothing else.

I have not been back to Tibet. I have been away a long time. I would like to go back to Tibet, but the problem is that I am not a Swiss citizen. I never applied for Swiss citizenship. When I was in the Pestalozzi Village many people asked me why I did not become a Swiss citizen and I said: 'Look, I have to teach children about Tibet and maintain their cultural heritage and I can't do that convincingly if I am a Swiss citizen.'

But now I have received many letters from people in Tibet asking me to visit. I am thinking about applying for Swiss citizenship and then, once I had it, I would be able to go. With Swiss citizenship I would have no problems in Tibet and I would not be harmed if I went back. But the Chinese would not make it easy for me because they know that my children are active in Tibetan exile politics and because I often write articles about Tibetan cultural and national identity. Without a Swiss passport it would be dangerous for me to go back because I have the name of a lama and because I was born into a military officer's family. Both these groups of people suffered terribly when the Chinese first invaded Tibet and during the Chinese Cultural Revolution they also had many problems. Many of my friends in Tibet were thrown into prison. If I had stayed behind I would have ended up there as well. I have two sisters still in Tibet and many friends too. Both of my sisters have had a hard time under the Chinese. One of my sisters is a very strong character and she refuses to accept communism and this caused her many difficulties.

If I did go back there is one thing I would not look forward to, however. My relatives and friends in Tibet have spent too much time under the Chinese – their minds are obsessed by the Chinese, about the problems they have had and how they have suffered. I am sure what they say is true, but after a while it is tiring. Before the Chinese invasion Tibetans were a happy-go-lucky people, but now so many have changed.

Notes

1. The *Kinderdorf Pestalozzi* (Pestalozzi Children's Village) was founded by the Swiss author and philosopher Walter Robert Corti in 1946. His aim was to take in refugee children from the war-ravaged countries of Europe and

to lay the basis for a better understanding between the nations of Europe. The name of the village is taken from the famous Swiss pedagogue Johann Heinrich Pestalozzi (1746–1827).

2. In 1959 several hundred thousand Tibetans fled Tibet after an uprising against Chinese troops in Lhasa was defeated. The uprising was the culmination of years of tension over Tibetan demands for political independence and Chinese claims of sovereignty.

3. The Dalai Lama is the spiritual leader of the Tibetan people who has lived in exile since 1960. He is the internationally-recognised leader of the Tibetan people but is not recognised by China.

Chapter 10

SWISS TRADITIONS: GUILDS AND *SCHWINGERS*

For a small country of close to seven million people, the Swiss pay an inordinate amount of attention to festivals, quaint customs and traditions. Whether it is the decapitation of a dead goose while blindfolded on St Martin's Day in the town square of Sursee, the three-day carnival procession which brings Basle (Switzerland's second largest city) to a standstill, or cow fights in the south-western canton of Valais to choose the season's queen cow, more likely than not some Swiss will be celebrating a local festival – based on a traditional activity – somewhere in Switzerland most weekends of the year.[1]

Among these traditions, Swiss wrestling, or *schwingen* as it is known among the German Swiss (*lutter* for the Francophone Swiss), is undoubtedly the most prominent. *Schwingen* is one of Switzerland's major sports, ranking alongside football, ice hockey and skiing in terms of the number of spectators it attracts. But unlike the other sports *schwingen*, together with the less widespread competitions of *hornussen* and boulder-heaving[2] which are often also held at *schwingen* festivals, is the only exclusively Swiss sport and its maintenance in its traditional form is fiercely guarded. Spectators sit on bare wooden planks or on the ground around a simple arena. The *schwingers*, heavy men wearing leather shorts over their trousers, fight in rings of sawdust laid down on the ground. They are all amateurs. Bouts usually last a maximum of eight minutes but can be extended to 15 minutes at important competitions. Scoreboards are made of wood and rotated by hand. Advertisement is forbidden and prizes are either laurel wreaths, cow bells or farm animals.

The exact origins of *schwingen* are not known, but it certainly existed several hundred years ago and may go as far back as the eleventh century. Probably it is attributable to shepherds and farmers who first began organising competitions and tests of strength at mountain festivals during the summer months. The name '*schwingen*' is believed to come from the way a fighter often lifts his opponent off the ground and then swings him (*schwingen*) around before throwing him on to his back and thudding down on top of him to pin his shoulders to the ground.

Schwingen bears a certain similarity to Graeco-Roman wrestling and to Japanese Sumo. However, in ancient Greek wrestling the competitors were naked and their bodies were oiled to make it more difficult for the opponent to get a grip. *Schwingen* has always allowed the fighters to grip each other's clothes; in fact, both fighters must have at least one hand gripping the leather shorts of their opponent and if they lose this grip the fight is interrupted.

Schwingen was banned at the start of the eighteenth century by the towns, who dominated the countryside politically and who regarded the fights as primitive and uncivilised. It was not revived until 1805 after the five-year Napoleonic occupation between 1798 and 1803 when the organisers – four Berne patrician families – hoped to repair the mistrust between town and country by supporting a festival of *schwingen*, boulder-throwing and alpenhorn-blowing in a place called Unspunnen in central Switzerland. The support in many Swiss villages for the invading French troops had worried the urban rulers and shown them how tenuous their control over the country was and they hoped that the Unspunnen games would generate a sense of Swiss national loyalty.

Gradually, during the nineteenth century townspeople began to take an interest in the sport and founded clubs and gymnasiums where they practised *schwingen* and other sports. This is the origin of the current very strict dress code. *Schwingers* are either dressed all in white, representing the town gymnasts, or they dress in dark colours usually with a chequered shirt, as the shepherds and farmers did in the nineteenth century. Today the distinction is no longer between town and country, but between exclusively *schwinger* clubs – the chequered shirts – and clubs which also cater to other sports, the white shirts.[3]

Critics argue *schwingen*, *hornussen* and boulder-heaving are nothing more than folklore – an artificial preservation of a so-called Swiss Alpine cultural heritage. The traditions are not genuine and would have died out long ago if it had not been for the particular attention paid to maintaining them. The criticism is not new. Swiss literary critic Emil Ermatinger wrote in 1933 that the 1805 Unspunnen games were a 'theatrical show of Swiss folklore [to] promote pure business interests'.[4]

While *schwingen* is a tradition for all of Switzerland, the guilds are an example of traditions operating on a much more local level. Although there is some limited guild activity in a number of Swiss cities, Zurich is the undisputed centre of guilds in Switzerland. Indeed Zurich's guilds, which once ruled the city, are the only ones in Europe to have grown in number over the last hundred years. Since 1866 the number of guilds in Zurich has more than doubled and five guilds have been founded in the last seven years. In Zurich every spring one of the city's most important ceremonies, the *Sechselaeuten* procession of guild members, is held.

Some see the guilds as a close-knit but harmless collection of people only interested in speeches, walking in the *Sechselaeuten* procession, and good food and drink. But others point out that they are a potent political club of the like-minded and economically influential. Membership is by invitation only and reserved for the sons and sons-in-law of existing members and for those who have achieved a certain status in society. It is said Jews and Catholics find less favour.

In this chapter Ueli Schlumpf, a former Swiss *schwinger* champion, explains what *schwingen* means to him and describes how the sport has changed since he won the national games in 1956. Reinhard von Meiss, a prominent authority on Zurich's guilds, gives a guild member's view of guilds and of the world.

Notes

1. The goose decapitation, or *Gaenseabhauet*, is held in the central Swiss town of Sursee on 11 November, St Martin's Day. Contestants are primed with a glass of red wine, blindfolded and then allowed one blow with a heavy double-handed sword at a dead goose suspended from a wire. The contestant who severs the head can keep the goose. The precise origins of the festival are not known, but it is believed to date from the Middle Ages when farmers sacrificed a hen or a goose in the hope that this would bring a good harvest the following year. An alternative theory is that the festival originated in the practice of landowners giving their tenants a goose after the tenants had paid their taxes.

The Basle carnival, or *Fasnacht*, is held at the beginning of the week following Ash Wednesday. Many of the floats or banners in the procession carry inscriptions poking fun at politicians or other public figures.

The cow fights are held in the spring and the autumn. They are between the Herens breed of cows, a small, black, aggressive strain which fight naturally for herd supremacy when they are on their alpine pastures in the summer. In the autumn contests cows must be in calf, while in the spring they must have calved in the previous 15 months.

2. *Hornussen* is a game in which competitors use a steel or graphite whip

to whiplash a puck down field where opponents try to block the puck's flight with large spade-shaped boards. In the boulder-heaving contests the competitor to throw a 83.5 kilogramme granite stone the farthest is the winner. *Hornussen* and boulder-heaving competitions are often held at larger *schwinger* festivals.

3. The confrontation between town and country is one of the core conflicts of early Swiss history and continues as a latent political tension to the present day. In the Middle Ages guilds in the towns excluded rural craftsmen from urban markets. As mentioned above, during the Napoleonic invasion and occupation people in the country welcomed the invaders for freeing them from the political yoke of the bourgeoisie in the towns. Later in the 1847 *Sonderbundkrieg*, Switzerland's only civil war, urban Protestant liberals fought rural Catholic conservatives. And the first Swiss federal constitution of 1848 was passed despite the opposition of many country dwellers.

4. Seiler (1993), p. 56. And to add to the controversy, in 1984 a separatist group from Francophone Switzerland, claiming that the Unspunnen Festival was an example of cultural imperialism by German-speaking Swiss over the rest of the country, stole the original boulder used in 1805. It has not been returned.

THE *SCHWINGER*

Ueli Schlumpf

Ueli Schlumpf's physique shows he was a wrestler. He is tall and heavily built, with slightly sagging jowls, and moves a little slowly because of a knee injury he suffered during a bout at the pinnacle of his career as a *schwinger*. He was forced to retire from fighting after the injury.

Schlumpf, 59, works in the city hall of the wealthy commune of Kuesnacht, just outside Zurich on the eastern shore of the lake. He tidies away a few documents into the various cabinets and drawers of his ground-floor office, before settling heavily into a chair behind his desk.

It is hot and he has closed the shutters of the windows in order to try and cool the room. But still he is perspiring heavily. 'Do you find it as warm as I do?' Periodically he reaches for a handkerchief that he has hung from a desk drawer and mops his forehead and face.

Occasionally Schlumpf is interrupted by a telephone call. He gives clipped, monosyllabic answers. He avoids getting up from his chair, which is on casters, but prefers to roll across the floor to get a piece of paper from the cupboard behind him. When visitors come to the office with a query he swivels and talks to them across the room from his desk rather than getting up to talk to them from the counter.

He is modest about his own achievements and is reluctant to talk about them, but smiles in appreciation and obvious pride when pressed.

My best period was 1956 when I won at the national games and was Swiss champion. I was a *schwinger* for a very short time. I had a very steep ascent to the top and an even steeper descent once I was there because of injury. But I achieved everything that can be achieved in *schwingen*. I won laurel wreaths at the cantonal games and at a couple of other games and finally at the national games; shortly after that it was all over. I was injured during a bout, a meniscus injury, and in those days they could not operate to repair it like they can now. My meniscus is okay now, but the ligaments are not.

The final bout which I won at the national games and which gave me the champion's title was a very evenly balanced fight. It lasted almost the full eight minutes. My opponent was Kurt Hagman from Solothurn. He was a head taller than me, but I was luckier. He always had bad luck. He twice fought at the national games for the winner's prize but lost both times.

Since my day the *schwingers* have neither improved nor got worse. It is the training methods, not the throws, that have changed. There used to be many more farmers who were *schwingers* and many more butchers and manual workers in general. And these people did not need much training for the games. I was a farmer and I did not need to do any extra jogging or jumping or anything like that. My training was at work, out in the fields and with the farm animals. It was the same for butchers who used to carry heavy carcasses of meat around all day. Today that has changed. We have more students, we have even had one *schwinger* champion who was an academic. They spend all day at a desk and, of course, they need to train, that's clear. But nothing has changed in the technique of *schwingen*.

One other thing that has changed is the weight of the *schwingers*. If you had put the *schwingers* at a national festival in 1920 on the scales and you weighed today's *schwingers*, you would find that the competitors are now lighter. We no longer have the 120 and 140 kilo colossuses of those times; the average weight now is around 100 kilos. I'm sure there are some exceptions and some of today's *schwingers* are also around 120 kilos, but most are not.

But you can't weigh much less than 100 kilos and be successful. If you want to be a *schwinger* you need a certain physique. There may be some athletes who only weigh 75 kilos and are still top *schwingers* but they are the exception. Most of them are around 95 to 100 kilos. You simply have to have this kind of constitution and the strength that goes with it to be able to lift your opponent – who will weigh around 100 kilos – off the ground and throw him on to the ground or, of course, to take being thrown yourself. You have got to be able to survive if someone weighing 100 kilos crashes down on top of you. Even though it's on sawdust it is still a pretty heavy weight.

The tactics and technique are what distinguish good and bad *schwingers* from each other. One *schwinger* might only master one or two throws and another wrestler many more; that varies widely. But it is the ability to move quickly at the right moment and to use your opponent's weight and body movement to throw him that is important.

My son was also a *schwinger*. He started when he was 16 and finished when he was 30. I have five laurel wreaths, he has 50. But he never won the national games and I always rib him about that. Whenever he says he has won more laurel wreaths than I did, I can always say that he never won at the national games. But winning at the national games is a question of luck. It often happens that a good *schwinger* never manages to win the national games. When I won I was only in the competition by chance because I had replaced another *schwinger* from my team who had had to pull out because of injury.

But in some ways *schwingen* has changed, and in a direction I don't like. It has become more commercial. Some of the prizes for the *schwingers* at the games have become too valuable in my opinion and there are also too many prizes. The sponsors are keen to give expensive prizes; I suppose it's a matter of prestige. But I think the prizes are too valuable now and it would be good if the prizes went back to being more symbolic.

I was at a festival last weekend in Schaffhausen and the first prize was a breeding ox, the second and third prizes were cows, and the fourth prize a boar. I think that is out of proportion; it's too much of a good thing. But there seem to be so many people who want to give prizes. At the national games we never have a problem finding donors for the prizes, in fact they compete with each other and bid against each other to offer the best prizes. This is despite them being unable to use the donation of these prizes in any advertisements or for marketing purposes.

Originally, of course, it made sense to have farm animals as prizes because the *schwingers* were mostly farmers. The farmer could take his prize home and thus increase his farm stock. In the 1920s the first prize at the national games was usually a sheep.

Later this was changed to a breeding ox. Now of course, with many of the *schwingers* no longer being farmers, these prizes have become rather inappropriate. They are still given, but unless the winner is a farmer he simply sells his prize, usually immediately after the festival. A breeding ox is usually worth between 3,000 and 6,000 francs. In fact, usually the sale of the prize has been agreed beforehand, and whoever donates the prize takes it back and hands over the value of the prize in cash. The animals are really only there for the photographers.

Of course, in a way it is understandable that there are more prizes now than before because the *schwingers* are not professionals and they need to find some way of covering the costs of participating in *schwingen* festivals. My son, for example, competed at about ten different *schwinger* festivals a year. But he only won a prize at about three and all the costs for the other seven were not covered by anyone. He had to pay the travel costs, the accommodation costs and so on himself.

Schwingen is not only an amateur sport, it is also the only sport in Switzerland that is not subsidised by the state. There is also virtually no money from advertising. The only place where advertisements are allowed is outside the arena. *Schwingers* are banned from using *schwingen* as a professional source of income. However, the question of advertisement is very controversial at the moment and has become a bit of a problem.

Everything is becoming more expensive every year and some of the regional *schwinger* associations argue that advertising should be allowed to help pay for the running of the games. At big national *schwinger* festivals the financing is not a problem, but at smaller ones it certainly is. But others say we would lose the traditional nature of *schwingen* if we started having Coca-Cola signs all over the place, and would end up having to change the games to suit the advertisers and sponsors. It is certainly true that we would have no problem getting sponsors and advertisers if we wanted them. *Schwingen* is an ideal sport for television and I am sure sponsors would jump at the chance of the advertising opportunities it would offer.

Berne and eastern Switzerland are more traditionalist on this question, while the French-speakers in western and north-western Switzerland are more open and welcome advertising. I have now reached the age where people tend to be very conservative and I belong to the traditionalists.

If more money was pumped into the sport through sponsors it would change the nature of the games and festivals. There is almost no sport in Switzerland where the members are so willing to work on a voluntary basis as in *schwingen*. We never have problems finding volunteers to organise and run the games. If these people were not volunteers but paid staff it would change the whole atmosphere.

Also if the *schwingers* could earn enough money from the sport to become professionals this would also completely change the games. We would lose the sense of fair play which is a very important part of *schwingen*. Every *schwinger* must shake his opponent's hand before and after each bout and the winner brushes the sawdust off the loser's back after the fight is over to show that there are no hard feelings. Although the scoring system can be very controversial, it never leads to protests or arguments. That would all change if there was serious money at stake.

We might even start seeing transfers of *schwingers* between clubs, and so on, which is not something we want. The way it works now a *schwinger* living in Berne can only be a member of a club in Berne and cannot fight for a club somewhere else in the country. There is no transfer market. If he moves to Zurich for personal or career reasons, then he has to change to a club there.

Schwingen seems to be gaining in popularity. We have no difficulty in attracting 40,000 spectators to a national *schwinger* festival. But even thirty years ago *schwingen* was popular. I remember how in 1974 we had the national games on the same Sunday as the final of the World Cup and everyone was worried that nobody would show up. But it was no problem, even Switzerland's most prominent football personality, the manager of Zurich's football club, came rather than watching the World Cup on television.

Some women have tried and succeeded in setting up *schwingen* competitions for women. They have founded a women's *schwinger* association. I think this is wrong and silly. I do not see anything wrong with a woman playing tennis or swimming, but playing football or *schwingen* – that's not attractive. I doubt it has a future. We are not enemies of women and we are happy if they want to help us at the *schwinger* festivals, selling sausages or whatever, but fighting with each other on the sawdust? That does not make sense.

GUILDS IN SWITZERLAND

Reinhard von Meiss

Reinhard von Meiss, a 53-year-old commercial lawyer, slightly balding, talks with a loud, booming voice and in a commanding manner. During the interview, at his home overlooking Lake Zurich, he sits in an easy chair in the lounge but frequently jumps up enthusiastically to get family silver or books from other rooms to illustrate what he is saying. At one point he pulls out a large, old guild certificate, stored in a box behind the sofa, and lovingly unpacks and displays it. His family has long been associated with guild life in Zurich.

The guilds in Zurich are exclusive clubs for the bourgeoisie and for men. We don't just let anyone in who shows an interest. The kind of people we accept as members are those of standing in Zurich, who have a connection with this city and who are interested in the success of Zurich. This attitude has existed since the foundation of the guilds around 700 years ago and it still exists today. In fact the guilds have become a haven, a kind of *reduit* for the bourgeoisie. It is interesting that the guilds, not only in Zurich, but in other Swiss towns and cities as well, have never been influenced by or turned to the political left wing.

The guilds in Switzerland have had an important impact on the country. They laid the foundations for the cartel thinking and organisation that is still very widespread in the Swiss economy and in the mentality of the Swiss people. This is only now beginning slowly to be dismantled. And the guilds are still important today. To understand this one must know a little about the history of the guilds.

The earliest guilds in Switzerland were founded in the twelfth century. They were organisations of craftsmen and artisans that developed throughout much of German-speaking Europe and in England. To become a master of a particular craft one had to pass a particular examination and one could only do this if one belonged to a guild. One could also only take on apprentices and junior craftsmen as employees if one was a member of a guild. Thus the guilds had a very strong influence over the way an individual's business was run. The control of the guilds was restricted to the town in which they were based and so before a master craftsman from one town could move into another and find work there, he had to become a member of the relevant guild.

The motive for founding many guilds was to preserve a craft for the members, for example to define the specifications of a plough and to prevent any idiot with poor knowledge of plough construction ruining the reputation of the craftsmen of a particular town by making bad ploughs. The protectionist efforts of the guilds were also directed against the rural population and aimed at preventing agrarian craftsmen developing.

Because the guilds controlled both employment and supply to the market, many of them gained ever greater political influence in their towns during the thirteenth and fourteenth centuries. Other conservative forces, mainly businessmen and traders and some nobles who dominated the town governments, tried to protect their interests and their power by restricting the guilds to the economic sphere. In Zurich, the *Grosser Rat* (executive council) strictly forbade any political activity by the guilds.

However, this did not prevent the guilds seizing power in Zurich, which was among the earliest Swiss towns where this happened. Wealthy merchants and traders, who had made their money particularly in the silk-weaving business and were buying up the lands and properties of the old, noble families in and around Zurich, had come to dominate the *Grosser Rat*. This led to tension and political battles for power between the wealthy merchants and traders on the one hand and the guilds on the other. In 1336 the craftsmen of Zurich rioted against the unpopular rule of the merchants. They stormed the town hall and forced the representatives of the hated merchants and traders to flee.

A new constitution for Zurich was passed which reorganised the guilds and laid down standards for them, including rules such as how many people were allowed to be employed in a shop, or whether foreign master craftsmen would be allowed into the town or a guild, and so on. The guilds now shared political power with the so-called *Gesellschaft zur Constaffel*, which was then made up of landowners and nobles.

The guilds changed and it became a matter of honour to be a member of a guild because the guilds had power. Originally the power had been that of the cartel with control over the particular craft, but after the 1336 uprising political power was added to this. The ties to the craft loosened and the guilds developed into groups similar to today's political parties. New members who were looking to join a guild saw membership as a path to political influence. A prospective member chose a guild appropriate to his political aims and aspirations for a position in the town government.

After the Napoleonic invasion of Switzerland the guilds lost their political power. Napoleon first removed them from government and then used them, under the Mediation Constitution,[1] to create election districts. Zurich was divided into five areas with each area separated into 13 so-called Land Guilds, or voting areas. Each of these Land Guilds sent one representative to the *Grosser Rat*, which in total had 195 representatives. One had to be a member of a guild to be able to vote. Thus by the end of the eighteenth century the political power of guilds had ceased to exist, although it was not until 1866 and the introduction of the new community law of the city of Zurich that the adult male population was given full voting rights and the last political rights of the guilds were abolished.

So how did the guilds continue in the nineteenth century after the Napoleonic reforms had deprived them of their cartel power and their institutionalised political power? Certain families kept their ties to their guilds – the father would pass on his membership to his sons. But for most of this period they ran close to extinction, perhaps only remaining alive because there was a guild house where hardy and faithful members could meet. Some guilds were little more than social clubs with a link to Zurich. In many respects they slightly lost their way, without targets or objectives, and the admission or membership criteria became very lax.

At some point late in the nineteenth century one of the guilds decided to participate in the annual Zurich *Sechselaeuten*[2] festival and marched in a procession at night and then afterwards visited some of the other guilds in the evening and delivered speeches. This was the beginning of the modern period for the guilds when one of their roles became to participate in public celebrations and festivals, always dressed in period costumes representing different periods in Zurich history. This role, and in particular the procession by the guilds at *Sechselaeuten*, has given the guilds a task – a meaning and something to hold them together. And that is probably one of the main reasons why the guilds in Zurich are so well-developed, active and numerous compared with guilds in other cities and towns – because they have a common activity.

The guilds' participation in *Sechselaeuten* may be a reason for their popularity, but the real source of their power lies in their bringing together like-minded bourgeois people who all share the same commitment to this city. This power is a latent strong political force because the guilds potentially have the means to mobilise a large number of often influential people to fight for certain issues and to sway public opinion. Of course the guilds do not have any formal political power, but they do enjoy a certain position of respect and authority.

There are some guild members who feel the guilds should exploit this potential power and actively participate in the politics of Zurich, take positions on political issues, and so on. And, of course, it is true that most of us in the guilds are not happy with the current left–green coalition in the city government. Quite a few guildmasters feel the guilds should participate actively in politics, particularly during the election campaigns. I see this as wrong. But this would not stop a guild taking such a step because every guild is independent – there is no parent organisation which the individual guilds are answerable to.

But my view is that the guilds of Zurich are at least 650 years old and have survived other socialist governments; they will manage to live through the rule of this government as well. If we were to take a more active and public political position we would fundamentally change the nature of the guilds and we would be drawn into the morass of politics rather than presenting a secure haven for the bourgeoisie.

It is true that we are rather a closed group and the possibilities for taking on new members are limited. Most guilds accept the eldest son of a member as a new member if there is nothing else that goes against him. If a newcomer, who does not have family ties to a guild member, is asked to join then, of course, he must be someone who has ties to Zurich and is of a bourgeois outlook.

There are 25 guilds plus the *Constaffel* in Zurich and they have between one hundred and twenty and two hundred members each, so that together there are around three to four thousand members in Zurich in total. People want to join the guilds because of the opportunities they offer for social and business contacts. The guilds today are like the Rotary Club, or many other groups. If you have two equally good candidates applying to you for a job and you discover one is a member of a group, say a guild, to which you also belong, then you are certain to choose that candidate because in some way you can fit the person into your picture of the world.

What I dislike is when some members try to use and exploit the contacts that membership offers. Recently someone asked me to invite a prominent person in Switzerland as our honorary guest to *Sechselaeuten*, saying that such an invitation would make a tremendous impact. I refused because the person was not one of us. His philosophy and views were not ours. We are not in the business of collecting business cards.

It is not true to say that Catholics have no chance of joining the guilds. However, in Zurich the Reformation under Huldrych Zwingli,[3] which was supported by many citizens, was also supported by the guilds and this laid the foundations for the Protestantism of the guilds which has continued to the present day. None of the guilds here requires its members to be Protestants but traditionally they have more Zwinglian Protestant roots than Catholic ones.

Jews, by and large, do not fit into the guilds; they have loyalties to their group and to other values, and not just to Zurich and the bourgeoisie. Of course, there are exceptions and there are some Jews who have become more Zuricher than the Zurichers. And there are some guilds that have Jewish members. We certainly do not make detailed investigations into the ethnic roots of applicants.

Women cannot join the guilds. We are societies of men – that has been the case historically and is still the case today. This is not something that one has to justify. If women want to participate in guild life perhaps they should found a women's guild.[4] But the great danger is that the women who would want to set up a guild would be driven by ideas of feminism and the desire to fight against male domination. And that is the wrong motivation. If women put their own personal ambitions so much in the forefront, then a women's guild will inevitably fail.

Notes

1. In 1798 Napoleon, after invading and defeating what little military opposition there was mainly by troops from Berne, imposed a very centralistic constitution on Switzerland dividing the country into 19 cantons and greatly limiting the wide autonomy of the previous 13 sovereign areas as well as numerous other communities – variously under the rule of foreign nobility, the Church, or also autonomous – loosely bound to the areas. This led to the abolition of many medieval practices such as torture, many taxes and duties, and also the closed shop of the guilds. It also led to the division of the country into the Federalists who wanted to return to the old system and the Unitarians or Centralists who preferred the system imposed by Napoleon. In 1803 the tensions in Switzerland were so great that Napoleon was forced to intervene in the country again and to impose the Mediation Constitution, which eased domestic tension but also greatly circumscribed cultural and educational freedoms.

2. *Sechselaeuten*: since the Second World War the *Sechselaeuten* ritual has been more or less fixed. On Sunday the costumed children's procession, on Monday the costumed procession of all guilds, in the evening at 18.00 precisely the execution of the *Boeoegg*. The *Boeoegg* is a cotton wool snowman filled with firecrackers, which is meant to symbolise the heathen celebration of the end of winter. The pyre is ignited once the bells of the Church of St Peter chime six. *Sechselaeuten* is always held on the third Monday in April unless it clashes with Easter Monday, in which case it is postponed one week. The name *Sechselaeuten* comes from the practice, believed to have originated in the thirteenth century, of workers in Zurich agreeing from the end of winter to work every day until the chimes of the bells for 6 o'clock. During the winter, when the days were short, they worked from dawn to dusk. In 1921 the *Boeoegg* was ignited and burnt too early on the day by a fanatical young communist. In desperation the whole town participated in constructing another *Boeoegg* which was ready by the requisite time of 18.00. The *Boeoegg* must be 3.4 metres high and weighs some 80 kg. *Sechselaeuten* is the only guild activity in the year which is carried out in public.

3. Huldrych Zwingli, 1484–1531, was one of the leading thinkers of the Reformation. He broke Zurich's ties to the Roman Catholic Church and was a major proponent of the Reformation in the Swiss cantons.

4. A women's guild does exist in Zurich, but it is not recognised by the other, male, guilds.

Zurich's Guilds

Original guilds

Gesellschaft zur Constaffel Original membership of landowners, nobles and traders, now has professors, lawyers, doctors, directors, politicians and high-ranking army officers as members, founded 1336.

Zunft zur Saffran Trade in textiles, ironware and particularly spices (saffron), 1336.

Zunft zur Meisen Winetrade, 1336.

Zunft zur Schmiden All blacksmiths, coppersmiths, goldsmiths, etc., 1336.

Zunft zum Weggen Millers and breadbakers, 1336.

Zuenfte zur Gerwe u. Schuhmachern Leather workers, tanners and cobblers, both 1336 and then merged into one guild in 1877.

Zunft zum Widder Butchers and livestock traders, still today has some 30 butcher members, 1336.

Zunft zur Zimmerleuten Carpenters, builders, wagon-makers, 1336.

Zunft zur Schneidern Tailors, 1336.

Zunft zur Schiffleuten Fishermen, sailors and land transport workers, 1336.

Zunft zum Kaembel Vegetable traders, dairy produce traders, fish traders, and beans and lentils trade, 1336.

Zunft zur Waag Wool trade, hatters, linen trade, 1336.

Young guilds (founded after 1866)

Stadtzunft Political members who lost membership following 1866 electoral reform and formed their own guild. Until introduction of universal male suffrage in 1866 many men were only members of guilds so that they could vote. Following the 1866 reform they were expelled from the guilds and then formed their own guild in 1867.

Zunft Riesbach From Riesbach, former suburb of Zurich, now part of city, founded 1887.

Zunft zu den Drei Koenigen From Enge, as above, 1897.

Zunft Fluntern From Fluntern, as above, 1897.

Zunft Hottingen From Hottingen, as above, 1897.

Zunft zu Wiedikon From Wiedikon, as above, 1897.

Zunft Wollishofen From Wollishofen, as above, 1900.

Zunft Hard From Aussersihl, as above, 1922.

Zunft zu Oberstrass Former suburb, 1925.

Zunft St Niklaus Three former suburbs, Oerlikon, Seebach, Affoltern, 1933.

Zunft Hoengg Former suburb, now part of city, 1934.

Zunft zur Letzi From former suburbs Altstetten and Albisrieden, now part of city, name from former defence lines of city of Zurich, 1934.

Zunft Schwamendingen Former suburb, now part of city, 1975.

Zunft Witikon As above, 1980.

BIBLIOGRAPHY

Altwegg, Juerg (1993) *Der Mann der sein Leben aus dem Handgelenk schuettelt: Nicholas Hayek*, Frankfurter Allegemaine Zeitung, August

Amstutz, Peter (1985) *Die Armee und die Schweiz – Joerg Zumstein im Gespraech mit Peter Amstutz*, Verlag Martin Michel AG, Freiburg

Auboin, Roger (1955) *Die Bank fuer Internationale Zahlungsausgleich 1930–55*, Bank for International Settlements, Basle, May

Baumann, Walter (1992) *Zuercher Sechselaeuten*, Verlag Neue Zuercher Zeitung, Zurich

Bertossa, Luca, Binzegger, Daniel and Buehler, Stefan (1994), 'Das gewicht der militaerischen ausbildung und Karriere', *Schweizerische Arbeitgeber-Zeitung*, 3, 20 January

Bihrer, Rudolf and Poltera, Reto (1990) *Zuerichs Zuenfte einst und Jetzt*, Verlag Hans Rohr, Zurich

Binkert, Janice and Warr, Simon (1990) 'The Jewish Community in Switzerland', *Swiss News*, No. 9, September

Duerrenmatt, Friedrich (1991) *Kants Hoffnung*, Diogenes Verlag, Zurich

Enz, Rudolf (1991) *Preise und Loehne rund um die Wett*, Union Bank of Switzerland, August

Ferdmann, Helga (1989) *Der andere Zauberberg*, Genossenschaft Davoser Revue, Davos

Flueeler, Niklaus and Gfeller-Corhesy, Roland (1975) *Die Schweiz*, Ex Libris Verlag, Zurich

Geo Special – Schweiz (1987), 1, 11 February, Verlag Gruner and Jahr AG, Hamburg

Haesler, Alfred (1992) *Das Boot ist voll*, Pendo Verlag, Zurich

Kamber, Peter (1993) *Schuesse auf die Befreier*, Rotpunkt Verlag, Zurich

Keller, Stefan (1993) *Grueningers Fall*, Rotpunkt Verlag, Zurich

Kopp, Elisabeth (1991) *Briefe*, Benteli-Werds Verlag AG, Berne

Kreis, Georg (ed.) (1993) *Staatsschutz in der Schweiz, Die Entwicklung von 1935–1990*, Verlag Paul Haupt, Berne

Le Carré, John (1991) *The Unbearable Peace*, Granta 35, Granta Publications, London

McKinsey and Company (1986) *Perspektiven fuer den Schweizerischen Privat-bankenmarkt*, Zurich, October

Maeder, Peter M. and Mattern, Guenter (1993) *Fahnen und Ihre Symbole*, Schweizerisches Landesmuseum

Mast, Hans J. (1990) *Kapitalflucht aus Entwicklungslaendern und die Schweiz, Jahrbuch Schweiz-Ditte Welt*

Mehr, Mariella (1981) *Steinzeit*, Zytglogge Verlag, Berne

Picard, Jacques (1993) 'Die Vermoegen rassisch, religioes und politisch Ver-folgter in der Schweiz und ihre Abloesung von 1946 bis 1973', Unpublished study commissioned by Lawrence Lever, financial editor of the *Mail on Sunday*, Berne, January

— (1994) *Die Schweiz und die Juden, 1933–1945*, Chronos Verlag, Zurich

Schloeth, Daniel (1994) 'Mit dem Jubilaeumsjahr kam das Mistrauen', *Tages-anzeiger*, 15 June

Schmitt, Pierre-André (1993) 'Der retter der Schweiz? Vielleicht!', *Schweizer Woche*, 16/93

Schwander, Marcel (1991) *Schweiz*, CH Beck'sche Verlagsbuchhandlung AG, Munich

Schweizer Bankier Vereinigung (1991/92) *Jahresbericht*, 80

— (1992/93) *Jahresbericht*, 81

Schweizerisches Landesmuseum (1992) *Sonderfall? Die Schweiz zwischen Reduit und Europa*, Schweizerisches Landesmuseum, Zurich

Seiler, Christian (1993) 'Die Tradition aus der Retorte', *Die Weltwoche*, No. 35, 2 September

Sieber, Pfarrer Ernst (1987) *Menschenware – Wahre Menschen*, Zytglogge Ver-lag, Berne

— (1991) *Platzspitz – Spitze des Eisbergs*, Zytglogge Verlag, Berne

Steinberg, Jonathan (1976) *Why Switzerland?*, Cambridge University Press, Cambridge

Taylor, William (1993) 'Message and muscle: an interview with Swatch titan Nicholas Hayek', *Harvard Business Review*, No. 93205, Boston, USA

Trepp, Gian (1993) *Bankgeschaefte mit dem Feind*, Rotpunktverlag, Zurich

Verzeichnis der Verwaltungsraete 1994 (1994) *Informationswerke*, Orell Fuessli Verlag, Zurich

Ziegler, Jean (1982) *Das Schweizer Imperium*, Rowohlt TaschenbuchVerlag GmbH, Reinbek bei Hamburg, June

INDEX